Vedic Mathematics
For Schools

Vedic Mathematics For Schools

JAMES T. GLOVER

Preface of

H.E. DR. L.M. SINGHVI

Formerly High Commissioner for India in the UK

BOOK 1

MOTILAL BANARSIDASS PUBLISHERS
PRIVATE LIMITED ● DELHI

First Edition: Delhi, 1995
Reprint: Delhi, 1997, 2000, 2002, 2004

ISBN: 81-208-1318-9

MOTILAL BANARSIDASS
41 U.A. Bungalow Road, Jawahar Nagar, Delhi 110 007
8 Mahalaxmi Chamber, 22 Bhulabhai Desai Road, Mumbai 400 026
236, 9th Main III Block, Jayanagar, Bangalore 560 011
120 Royapettah High Road, Mylapore, Chennai 600 004
Sanas Plaza, 1302 Baji Rao Road, Pune 411 002
8 Camac Street, Kolkata 700 017
Ashok Rajpath, Patna 800 004
Chowk, Varanasi 221 001

Printed in India
BY JAINENDRA PRAKASH JAIN AT SHRI JAINENDRA PRESS,
A-45 NARAINA, PHASE-I, NEW DELHI-110 028
AND PUBLISHED BY NARENDRA PRAKASH JAIN FOR
MOTILAL BANARSIDASS PUBLISHERS PRIVATE LIMITED.
BUNGALOW ROAD, DELHI 110 007

Preface by
His Excellency Dr L.M.Singhvi
High Commissioner for India in the UK

Vedic Mathematics for Schools is an exceptional book. It is not only a sophisticated pedagogic tool but also an introduction to an ancient civilisation. It takes us back to many millennia of India's mathematical heritage. Rooted in the ancient Vedic sources which heralded the dawn of human history and illumined by their erudite exegeses, India's intellectual, scientific and aesthetic vitality blossomed and triumphed not only in philosophy, physics, ecology and performing arts but also in geometry, algebra and arithmetic. Indian mathematicians gave the world the numerals now in universal use. The crowning glory of Indian mathematics was the invention of zero and the introduction of decimal notation without which mathematics as a scientific discipline could not have made much headway. It is noteworthy that the ancient Greeks and Romans did not have the decimal notation and, therefore, did not make much progress in the numerical sciences. The Arabs first learnt the decimal notation from Indians and introduced it into Europe. The renowned Arabic scholar, Alberuni or Abu Raihan, who was born in 973 A.D. and travelled to India, testified that the Indian attainments in mathematics were unrivalled and unsurpassed. In keeping with that ingrained tradition of mathematics in India, S.Ramanujan, "the man who knew infinity", the genius who was one of the greatest mathematicians of our time and the mystic for whom "a mathematical equation had a meaning because it expressed a thought of God", blazed many new mathematical trails in Cambridge University in the second decade of the twentieth century even though he did not himself possess a university degree.

The real contribution of this book, *Vedic Mathematics for Schools*, is to demonstrate that Vedic mathematics belongs not only to an hoary antiquity but is any day as modern as the day after tomorrow. What distinguishes it particularly is that it has been fashioned by British teachers for use at St James Independent Schools in London and other British schools and that it takes its inspiration from the pioneering work of the late Bharati Krishna Tirthaji, a former Sankarcharya of Puri, who reconstructed a unique system on the basis of ancient Indian mathematics. The book is thus a bridge across centuries, civilisations, linguistic barriers and national frontiers.

Vedic mathematics was traditionally taught through aphorisms or *Sutras*. A *Sutra* is a thread of knowledge, a theorem, a ground norm, a repository of proof. It is formulated as a proposition to encapsulate a rule or a principle. A single *Sutra* would generally encompass a wide and varied range of particular

v

applications and may be likened to a programmed chip of our computer age. These aphorisms of Vedic mathematics have much in common with aphorisms which are contained in Panini's *Ashtadhyayi*, that grand edifice of Sanskrit grammar. Both Vedic mathematics and Sanskrit grammar are built on the foundations of rigorous logic and on a deep understanding of how the human mind works. The methodology of Vedic mathematics and of Sanskrit grammar help to hone the human intellect and to guide and groom the human mind into modes of logical reasoning.

I hope that *Vedic Mathematics for Schools* will prove to be an asset of great value as a pioneering exemplar and will be used and adopted by discerning teachers throughout the world. It is also my prayer and hope that the example of St James Independent Schools in teaching Vedic mathematics and Sanskrit may eventually be emulated in every Indian school.

London
13th March 1995

Introduction

Vedic mathematics is a new and unique system based on simple rules and principles which enable mathematical problems of all kinds to be solved easily and efficiently. The methods and techniques are based on the pioneering work of the late Bharati Krishna Tirthaji, Sankarcarya of Puri, who established the system from the study of ancient Vedic texts coupled with a profound insight into the natural processes of mathematical reasoning.

The characteristic of Vedic mathematics is to present the subject as a unified body of knowledge and so reduce the burden and toil which young students often experience during their studies. It is based on sixteen principles which lie behind short rules of working, or aphorisms, which are easily remembered. In the Vedic system these aphorisms are called sūtras, simple terse statements expressing rules, definitions or governing principles. In some topics, the sūtras provide rules for special cases as well as for the general case. Understanding their nature and scope is achieved by the practice of their applications.

Experience of teaching the Vedic methods to children has shown that a high degree of mathematical ability can be attained from an early age while the subject is enjoyed for its own merits.

This book should be taken as an introductory volume. Many of the methods are developed further at a later stage and so, in the present text, it may not be apparent why a particular method is being given. An important characteristic is that, although there are general methods for calculations and algebraic manipulations, there are also methods for particular types of calculations. For example, specifically in multiplying and dividing numbers close to a base of ten, a hundred, a thousand, etc. Where such particular methods are introduced at an early stage it is because they relate to more general aspects of the system at a later stage or are simply very quick and easy ways to obtain answers.

The current methods of calculating which have been adopted by most schools are 'blanket' methods. For example, with division, only one method is taught and actually used by the children. Although it will suffice in all cases it may often be difficult to use. The Vedic system teaches three basic algorithms for division which are applied to meet the particular need in hand although each could be used for any division sum. The principle is that, if a particular sum can be done by an easier method, then that method should be used. Of course, with children, some mastery of the different methods must be accomplished before this more creative approach can be adopted. A simple example to illustrate this point is the method for finding the product of 19 and 7. The conventional system teaches us to multiply the 7 by 9, to get 63 and then to multiply 7 by 10 to get 70. On summing these we arrive at the answer of 133. The Vedic system is to look at the sum and say 7 times 20 is 140; 140 less 7 is 133. Bright children will arrive at this method for themselves but the Vedic mathematics teaches this sort of approach systematically.

The study of number begins at one which is an expression of unity. From here all the other numbers arise and if it were not for the number one we would not have any numbers at all. If there is any fear of large numbers it is always comforting to remember that there are really only nine together with nought which stands for nothing. All other numbers are just repetitions of these nine. It is useful to treat these nine numbers as friends. In fact, they are universal friends because everybody uses them every day in one way or another.

Vedic mathematics readily acknowledges the importance of the number one. Many calculations are made simple and easy by relating the numbers involved back to one. The very first sūtra or formula in Vedic Mathematics does just this. It relates every number to unity.

In Vedic mathematics there are sixteen sūtras or formulae and about thirteen sub-sūtras. The word sūtra (pronounced 'sootra') is from ancient India and means a thread of knowledge. The English word 'suture' comes from sūtra and a suture is the thread doctors use to stitch wounds together. The mathematical sūtras are short and simple statements which give formulae for how to answer mathematical problems. Each sūtra has a large number of uses at all levels of mathematics.

In the research work which has resulted in this course there have been two guiding maxims. The first is that there are only nine numbers, together with a nought, and that these numbers represent the nine Elements as described in the ancient scriptural texts of India. It is well known that the nine numerals and the nought originated in India but the philosophical tradition of the Hindus also ascribes a universal significance to each of the numbers. The second is that the whole of mathematics is governed by the sixteen sūtras, or short formula-like aphorisms, which are both objective and subjective in their character. They are objective in that they may be applied to solve everyday problems. The subjective aspect is that a sūtra may also describe the way the human mind naturally works. The whole emphasis of the system is on the process and movement taking place in the mind at the time that a problem is being solved. The effect of this is to bring the attention into the present moment.

Vedic Mathematics for Schools Book 1 is a first text designed for the young mathematics student of about eight years of age. The text introduces new and quick methods in numerical calculation and comprehension.

New algorithms used for numerical calculations are introduced and exercises are carefully graded to enable the distinct developmental steps of each method to be mastered. Each algorithm is denoted by a simple rule which, when applied and practised, provides a high standard of mathematical capability. The text incorporates explanations and worked examples of all the methods used and includes descriptions of how to set out written work.

The course has been written for children who, at the age of about eight, have mastered the basic four rules including times tables. Although this is assumed, it is also clear that at this stage the child needs a good deal of revision work in the basics as an on-going practice and this has been taken into account in the composing of exercises. Older children and even adults may also find the techniques interesting and useful. The text provides introductory steps to each Vedic algorithm which may be followed by pupils of the intended age level with some help from an adult.

The main emphasis at this stage is on developing numeracy which is the most essential aspect of mathematics. The text concentrates on these areas of mathematics and treats them as the core curriculum of the subject The main Vedic methods used in this book are those for multiplication, division and subtraction. These are further developed at a later stage in the course. Introductions to vulgar and decimal fractions, elementary algebra and vinculums are are also given. Topics in geometry, weights and measures and statistics are. not included in this text.

Experience has shown that children benefit most from their own practice and experience rather than being continually provided with explanations of mathematical concepts The explanations given in this text show the pupil how to practise so that they may develop their own understanding. It is also felt that teachers might provide their own practical ways of demonstrating this system or of enabling children to practice and experience the various methods and concepts.

It is assumed that pupils using this book already have a degree of mathematical ability. In particular, the times tables need to be fully established. The Vedic system relies on and develops mental capabilities and many of the answers to questions are obtained in only one line. This reliance is greatly aided by regular practice of mental arithmetic.

Only five of the sixteen sūtras and thirteen sub-sūtras are used in this book. Others will be introduced in later volumes.

1. All from nine and the last from ten	Nikhilam Navataścaraman Daśatah
2. Vertically and Crosswise	Urdhva Tiryagbhyām
3. Transpose and Adjust	Parāvartya Yojayet
4. By Elimination and Retention	Lopana Sthāpanābhyām
5. By one more than the one before	Ekādhikena Pūrvena

Note on pronunciation of Sanskrit:

a is long a, as in hark; **ś** is pronounced 'sh' (palatal) as in Fishguard;
v is labial w; **c** is pronounced 'ch' (palatal) as in church.

CONTENTS

Chapter One - Simple Practice of Number

Numbers

Number begins at One which is Absolute. All other numbers come from One but in fact there are only nine numbers and a nought. As long as we remember that there are only nine numbers and a nought then there need be no fear of large numbers. The nine numbers are our friends and we can play with them and use them to discover about the world in which we live.

Place Value

Because there are only nine numbers and a nought we count in groups of ten. And at ten the one which is Absolute stands with the unmanifest, nought, by its side. The first place value is that of units.

> Ten units make a TEN.
> Ten tens make a HUNDRED.
> Ten hundreds make a THOUSAND.

The names we use for the first seven place values are: UNITS, TENS, HUNDREDS, THOUSANDS, TEN-THOUSANDS, HUNDRED-THOUSANDS and MILLIONS.

In any number the value of a digit depends upon its position. For example, the two in 26 stands for two tens, whereas the two in 52 stands for two units.

To find the value of a digit in a number we look at the column in which that digit is placed. For example, the value of the digit 5 in 352 is five tens, because it is in the tens column.

Exercise 1a Give the value of 5 in the following:-
  (The answer to the first question is 5 units)

1. 35	6. 530	11. 5432	16. 43521
2. 15	7. 350	12. 1985	17. 94857
3. 53	8. 245	13. 3587	18. 58780
4. 125	9. 4566	14. 125004	19. 15362
5. 156	10. 1522	15. 856743	20. 276511

Exercise 1b Write the following numbers in words:

Example **A** Thirty-five.

	Thousands	Hundreds	Tens	Units
A			3	5
B			7	2
C			6	1
D		3	4	5
E		6	0	7
F	4	3	9	2

	Thousands	Hundreds	Tens	Units
G	1	4	2	6
H	5	7	8	9
I	4	2	4	5
J	5	6	0	0
K	9	0	0	3
L	1	3	2	8

Exercise 1c Write the following numbers in words:-

	Millions	100 Thousands	10 Thousands	Thousands	Hundreds	Tens	Units
A					3	5	4
B					4	1	7
C					9	8	0
D				6	5	0	3
E				9	8	7	6
F				5	0	3	2
G				3	2	0	1
H				7	8	7	9
I				1	6	5	4
J			1	1	3	4	7
K			5	6	2	1	4
L			9	9	9	9	9
M		1	1	3	5	0	6
N		3	1	2	5	4	6
O		2	3	6	0	0	1
P	3	2	6	5	0	8	7
Q	6	2	0	6	4	6	1

Exercise 1d Write the following numbers in words:

1. 12	**11.** 243	**21.** 5463	**31.** 76852
2. 38	**12.** 506	**22.** 7658	**32.** 40006
3. 42	**13.** 781	**23.** 6000	**33.** 57003
4. 57	**14.** 154	**24.** 7002	**34.** 50304
5. 87	**15.** 456	**25.** 4056	**35.** 89654
6. 54	**16.** 670	**26.** 4205	**36.** 8600
7. 25	**17.** 405	**27.** 2803	**37.** 42000
8. 77	**18.** 920	**28.** 8930	**38.** 451003
9. 99	**19.** 571	**29.** 1455	**39.** 768307
10. 101	**20.** 665	**30.** 9897	**40.** 8920043

Exercise 1e Write the following numbers in figures:

1. nineteen	**21.** nine hundred and twenty
2. forty-two	**22.** seven hundred and twenty one
3. fifty-eight	**23.** four hundred and thirty-seven
4. seventy-three	**24.** three hundred and fourteen
5. ninety-five	**25.** six hundred and forty-eight
6. sixty-eight	**26.** two hundred and seventy-three
7. thirty-one	**27.** three hundred and sixty-six
8. eighty-two	**28.** one thousand, five hundred
9. twelve	**29.** eight thousand and twenty-nine
10. twenty-nine	**30.** six thousand and twelve
11. six hundred	**31.** one thousand, two hundred
12. one hundred and nine	**32.** three thousand and forty-two
13. two hundred and fifty	**33.** two hundred and eight
14. five hundred and sixty	**34.** four thousand six hundred
15. three hundred and one	**35.** nine thousand and twenty-nine
16. eight hundred and nine	**36.** ten thousand, four hundred
17. Five hundred	**37.** twenty-five thousand
18. one hundred and eleven	**38.** nine hundred thousand
19. six hundred and fourteen	**39.** six million
20. nine hundred and thirty	**40.** four million, three hundred and thirty-two thousand

3

Patterns in number

Exercise 1f Look at the following numbers and write down the next two numbers in each pattern:

1. 1, 2, 3, 4, 5,...
2. 2, 4, 6, 8,....
3. 1, 3, 5, 7,...
4. 6, 9, 12, 15,...
5. 20, 22, 24, 26,...
6. 31, 33, 35, 37,...
7. 16, 19, 22, 25,...
8. 21, 25, 29, 33,...
9. 10, 20, 30, 40,...
10. 24. 36, 48, 60,...

11. 100, 90, 80, 70,...
12. 34, 40, 46,...
13. 75, 100, 125, 150,...
14. 20, 40, 60, 80,...
15. 29, 27, 25, 23,...
16. 105, 110, 115, 120,...
17. 8, 16, 24, 32,...
18. 27, 36, 45, 54,...
19. 0, 1, 3, 6, 10,...
20. 0, 2, 6, 14, 30,...

Addition and subtraction

Exercise 1g Addition and subtraction: write answers only.

1. $1 + 3 + 7$
2. $5 + 6 + 3$
3. $4 + 22 + 1$
4. $7 + 8 + 9$
5. $1 + 3 + 5 + 7$
6. $4 + 5 + 2 + 2$
7. $7 + 6 + 2$
8. $6 + 2 + 9$
9. $6 + 6 + 6$
10. $8 + 7 + 6 + 5$

11. $7 - 3 + 2$
12. $9 - 1 + 6$
13. $27 + 3 - 5$
14. $56 + 2 + 3$
15. $70 - 3$
16. $24 + 5 - 2$
17. $44 - 8$
18. $23 - 3 - 3$
19. $41 - 8 - 3$
20. $1 + 4 + 5 + 6$

21. $23 + 10$
22. $23 + 9$
23. $46 + 10$
24. $46 + 9$
25. $52 + 10$
26. $52 + 9$
27. $66 + 10$
28. $66 + 9$
29. $34 + 10$
30. $34 + 9$

31. $76 - 10$
32. $76 - 9$
33. $24 - 10$
34. $24 - 9$
35. $78 - 10$
36. $78 - 9$
37. $134 - 10$
38. $134 - 0$
39. $356 - 10$
40. $356 - 9$

Exercise 1h Addition with carrying

1. 45 + 24	**11.** 342 + 732	**21.** 2341 + 9031	**31.** 561 + 858
2. 67 + 28	**12.** 102 + 466	**22.** 6402 + 4500	**32.** 240 + 714
3. 49 + 57	**13.** 78 + 176	**23.** 543 + 8656	**33.** 4001 + 9031
4. 8 + 46	**14.** 354 + 800	**24.** 1200 + 3256	**34.** 8681 + 9937
5. 26 + 38	**15.** 489 + 32	**25.** 5690 + 659	**35.** 49 + 1736
6. 82 + 79	**16.** 253 + 45	**26.** 4657 + 6009	**36.** 8784 + 5092
7. 37 4 + 50	**17.** 223 322 + 454	**27.** 6024 1355 + 2042	**37.** 278 809 + 52
8. 39 49 + 18	**18.** 123 245 + 332	**28.** 5157 123 + 56	**38.** 553 898 + 112
9. 24 36 + 67	**19.** 234 321 + 538	**29.** 6700 768 + 1004	**39.** 56 837 + 16
10. 28 38 + 36	**20.** 245 366 + 314	**30.** 769 8760 + 9687	**40.** 997 354 + 444

Exercise 1i Write answers only

1. 24 + 7	**6.** 23 + 7	**11.** 156 + 7
2. 46 + 5	**7.** 67 + 5	**12.** 465 + 9
3. 58 + 3	**8.** 87 + 4	**13.** 357 + 5
4. 65 + 7	**9.** 29 + 7	**14.** 248 + 6
5. 98 + 3	**10.** 18 + 8	**15.** 565 + 6

Exercise 1j Easy Subtraction. Write answers only.

1.	23 – 11	**11.**	456 – 321	**21.**	7564 – 1212
2.	37 – 16	**12.**	444 – 223	**22.**	3409 – 1208
3.	48 – 24	**13.**	787 – 243	**23.**	4548 – 232
4.	23 – 12	**14.**	578 – 103	**24.**	6570 – 460
5.	78 – 46	**15.**	499 – 300	**25.**	8799 – 4002
6.	87 – 25	**16.**	654 – 33	**26.**	5657 – 1234
7.	56 – 26	**17.**	288 – 46	**27.**	6009 – 2008
8.	89 – 60	**18.**	867 – 16	**28.**	3216 – 15
9.	87 – 43	**19.**	768 – 157	**29.**	6758 – 37
10.	43 – 21	**20.**	466 – 265	**30.**	76859 – 2345

Exercise 1k Write answers only

1. 20 – 7	**6.** 23 – 5	**11.** 150 – 4
2. 40 –8	**7.** 62 – 5	**12.** 461 – 2
3. 51 – 3	**8.** 83 – 4	**13.** 300 – 5
4. 62 – 4	**9.** 21 – 7	**14.** 250 – 6
5. 90 – 3	**10.** 12 – 9	**15.** 500 – 6

Multiplication practice

Exercise 11 Oral

	2 × 3	3 × 6	0 × 1	7 × 8
	5 × 4	10 × 9	4 × 10	1 × 1
A	8 × 3	8 × 6	10 × 1	5 × 6
	3 × 4	9 × 2	9 × 3	8 × 9
	5 × 8	4 × 7	5 × 5	10 × 10

	9 × 1	3 × 3	2 × 7	0 × 9
	0 × 7	4 × 0	5 × 9	6 × 2
B	8 × 5	6 × 4	10 × 4	9 × 9
	6 × 6	10 × 8	4 × 2	7 × 4
	9 × 4	1 × 6	6 × 6	3 × 10

	3 × 1	0 × 5	6 × 0	4 × 1
	8 × 0	4 × 6	3 × 10	8 × 8
C	5 × 1	7 × 7	4 × 9	6 × 9
	3 × 7	6 × 10	7 × 5	0 × 0
	2 × 9	2 × 2	2 × 8	1 × 0

	2 × 4	2 × 0	6 × 1	4 × 3
	3 × 9	5 × 10	9 × 5	2 × 6
D	7 × 10	10 × 0	8 × 7	5 × 2
	6 × 8	4 × 8	9 × 8	7 × 3
	7 × 8	6 × 3	10 × 5	9 × 6

	6 × 7	12 × 10	0 × 3	2 × 12
	11 × 5	8 × 11	8 × 12	8 × 2
E	0 × 6	3 × 5	3 × 8	11 × 4
	1 × 11	2 × 9	4 × 12	5 × 12
	7 × 9	12 × 7	11 × 7	6 × 5

Division practice

Exercise 1m Oral

	3 into 12	7 into 7	1 into 8	3 into 9
	5 into 30	4 into 32	9 into 36	5 into 10
A	7 into 56	6 into 54	4 into 28	7 into 21
	4 into 16	4 into 24	5 into 15	10 into 40
	2 into 18	7 into 28	2 into 8	8 into 64
	3 into 6	4 into 4	3 into 21	5 into 25
	2 into 6	6 into 30	6 into 42	2 into 0
B	6 into 6	5 into 5	7 into 42	6 into 12
	1 into 6	7 into 35	2 into 14	8 into 24
	7 into 14	8 into 16	4 into 20	7 into 49
	8 into 32	6 into 24	4 into 40	3 into 27
	3 into 15	9 into 45	8 into 72	4 into 12
C	6 into 48	2 into 20	5 into 20	8 into 56
	4 into 36	6 into 18	3 into 0	7 into 63
	5 into 35	8 into 40	9 into 54	6 into 36

Divide

	20 by 2	12 by 6	27 by 9	48 by 6
	25 by 5	35 by 5	60 by 10	72 by 9
D	8 by 4	18 by 9	4 by 4	49 by 7
	15 by 3	40 by 5	12 by 2	45 by 5
	35 by 7	56 by 8	27 by 3	10 by 1
	$6 \div 3$	$81 \div 9$	$10 \div 2$	$44 \div 11$
	$36 \div 6$	$63 \div 7$	$6 \div 1$	$60 \div 12$
E	$14 \div 2$	$48 \div 8$	$16 \div 8$	$96 \div 12$
	$45 \div 9$	$18 \div 6$	$24 \div 2$	$99 \div 11$
	$42 \div 6$	$2 \div 2$	$36 \div 4$	$20 \div 1$

Chapter Two - Multiplication by Nikhilam

What is multiplication?

When any number is multiplied by one there is no change. For example, $4 \times 1 = 4$, $271 \times 1 = 271$. It is only when there is two or more that there can be any increase. This is indicated in the book of Genesis where God created male and female, that is two, before there could be any multiplication.

> So God created man in his own image, in the image of God created he him; male and female created he them.
>
> And God blessed them, and God said unto them, Be fruitful and multiply, and replenish the earth, and subdue it:

[Genesis 1:27-28]

In the story of Noah's Ark, after the great flood had subsided, God said to Noah,

> Be ye fruitful, and multiply; bring forth abundantly in the earth, and multiply therein.

Nature is very good at multiplication! Whatever else plants or creatures can do they can always increase by giving birth to baby plants and creatures, their 'children'. Some plants and creatures produce thousands of young ones whilst others only produce a few. All this comes from how good they are at multiplying.

When we multiply one number by another then it is increased and becomes further away from one. For example, when 2 is multiplied by 3 it becomes 6 which is further away from 1 than 2.

In this chapter we will be using complements to do multiplication. A complement is that which relates a number to unity. In mathematics the unity is expressed as 1 or 10 or 100, or 1 with any other number of noughts after it.

For the numbers relating to 10,

the complement of 9 is 1,
the complement of 8 is 2,
the complement of 7 is 3,
the complement of 6 is 4, etc.

Complements

The first Vedic sutra, to be used is, **Nikhilam Navataścaraman Daśatah**, which means,

All from nine and the last from ten.

This simple formula relates any number back to unity, or One. It does this by giving what must be added to the number to make it up to the next base of ten above.

For example, with the number 86, the nearest base of ten which is more than 86 is 100. If we take all from nine and the last from ten we have ,

$$8 \text{ from } 9 = 1$$
$$6 \text{ from } 10 = 4$$

86 is 14 less than 100. 14 is called the **complement** of 86.

To obtain the complement of	783	7 from 9 = 2
783 we take each of the digits	217	8 from 9 = 1
from 9 and the last from ten.		3 from 10= 7

When there are noughts at the end, the last number is taken from ten (nought is not a number). For example, the complement of 740 is 260, that is, 7 from 9 = 2, 4 from 10 = 6, and the nought is just added at the end. The meaning of the formula is All from nine and the last number from ten.

Exercise 2a   Write down the complements of the following:

1.	87	**11.**	874	**21.**	27463
2.	94	**12.**	426	**22.**	354600
3.	36	**13.**	903	**23.**	70603
4.	42	**14.**	1340	**24.**	99992
5.	88	**15.**	3564	**25.**	5003400
6.	75	**16.**	8004	**26.**	123980
7.	64	**17.**	30460	**27.**	453601
8.	28	**18.**	8638	**28.**	364720
9.	44	**19.**	1111	**29.**	2758407
10.	73	**20.**	38730	**30.**	6666667

Multiplication of single digit numbers

Some multiplications are made very easy using the sutra,

All from nine and the last from ten.

The first type of multiplication is where both numbers consist of a single digit and both are a little less than ten. The following example will show how this works. Suppose we have to multiply 7 × 8.

---

1   We should take 10 as the base of our calculation because it is the nearest unity to the numbers to be multiplied. We put the two numbers 7 and 8 above and below as shown and write the base, 10, above.

$$\begin{array}{r} (10) \\ 7 \\ \times\,8 \end{array}$$

2   Subtract each of them from the base ten to obtain the complements (2 and 3) and put these down on the right-hand side with a connecting minus sign. The minus sign shows that the complements are both **less** than 10.

$$\begin{array}{r} (10) \\ 7 - 3 \\ \times\,8 - 2 \end{array}$$

3   The answer will have two parts; a right-hand part and a left hand part. To distinguish these two parts we put a diagonal stroke underneath the minus signs, as shown.

$$\begin{array}{r} (10) \\ 7 - 3 \\ \times\,8 - 2 \\ \hline / \end{array}$$

4   The left-hand part of the answer is most easily found by *cross-subtraction*, either 7 − 2 = 5 or 8 − 3 = 5. Both give the same answer and you may choose whichever is the easiest. There are, in fact, four ways of arriving at this part of the answer. The other two are
     a) 7 + 8 − 10 (the base) = 5
and b) 10 (the base) − 2 − 3 = 5

$$\begin{array}{r} (10) \\ 7 - 3 \\ \times\,8 - 2 \\ \hline 5\,/ \end{array}$$

5   The right-hand part of the answer is to vertically multiply the two complement digits, 3 × 2 = 6. The answer is 56.

$$\begin{array}{r} (10) \\ 7 - 3 \\ \times\,8 - 2 \\ \hline 5\,/\,6 \end{array}$$

This method holds good in all cases. It is said that a very long time ago, the process of cross-subtraction actually gave rise to the × sign being used for multiplication. The diagram on the next page shows all the steps:

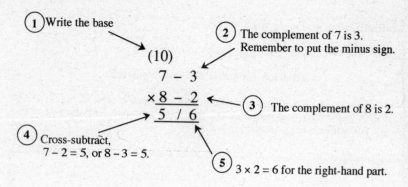

① Write the base

② The complement of 7 is 3.
Remember to put the minus sign.

(10)

7 – 3

× 8 – 2

5 / 6

③ The complement of 8 is 2.

④ Cross-subtract,
7 – 2 = 5, or 8 – 3 = 5.

⑤ 3 × 2 = 6 for the right-hand part.

Exercise 2b   Set these out as shown and answer them.

1.	9	3.	6	5.	9	7.	5	9.	9
	× 8		× 9		× 7		× 9		× 9

2.	8	4.	8	6.	8	8.	7	10.	9
	× 8		× 7		× 6		× 7		× 4

Multiplication using a base of 100

We can easily extend this method to multiplying big numbers. To start with we shall multiply two numbers which are close to 100, such as 97 and 94. The base will then be 100 and not 10.

Because we are going to use a base of 100 there will be two complement digits for each number. For example, when multiplying 97 by 94, we need to find the complement of 97, that is 03, and the complement of 94, that is 06. To find these complements we use the *All from nine and the last from ten* rule.

So for 97, 9 from 9 is 0 and 7 from 10 is 3. The complement is therefore 03.

For 94, 9 from 9 is 0 and 4 from 10 is 6. This gives 06 as the complement.

From there on the method is exactly the same as before; multiply the complements for the right-hand part of the answer and cross-subtract for the left-hand part.

This example is shown on the next page.

1	Suppose we need to multiply 97 by 94. As before we write the base, this time 100, above and set the sum out as shown.	(100) 97 × 94
2	To obtain the complement of 97, using *All from nine and the last from ten*, 9 from 9 = 0 and 7 from 10 = 3, which gives 03 to be put down on the right with the connecting minus sign. Again using the Nikhilam rule, the complement of 94 is 06.	(100) 97 – 03 × 94 – 06 /
3	Cross-subtract for the left-hand part of the answer; 97 – 06 = 91 or 94 – 03 = 91	(100) 97 – 03 × 94 – 06 91 /
4	Multiply 3 and 6 for the right-hand part of the answer, 3 × 6 = 18.	(100) 97 – 03 × 94 – 06
5	The answer is 9118.	91 / 18

Exercise 2c Multiply using base 100:

1. 94 × 98	7. 98 × 98	13. 92 × 99	19. 94 × 99	25. 96 × 99	
2. 98 × 91	8. 93 × 99	14. 93 × 98	20. 92 × 98	26. 77 × 98	
3. 92 × 97	9. 97 × 98	15. 96 × 96	21. 94 × 97	27. 95 × 96	
4. 96 × 97	10. 95 × 99	16. 95 × 97	22. 91 × 97	28. 93 × 96	
5. 99 × 99	11. 91 × 99	17. 92 × 96	23. 88 × 96	29. 98 × 88	
6. 98 × 99	12. 96 × 98	18. 95 × 98	24. 81 × 98	30. 97 × 89	

Multiplication using a base of 1000

Multiplication by Nikhilam can easily be extended to bigger bases. Since there are now three noughts in the base, there must be three digits on the right-hand side

$$
\begin{array}{ll}
786 \times 998 & (1000) \\
& 786 - 214 \\
& \times\ 998 - 002 \\
\hline
& 784\ /\ 428
\end{array}
$$

It is worth pointing out a rule concerning the number of digits in the complements on the right. This is given in a short rhyme:

The number of digits in the complement's case
is the same as the number of noughts in the base.

In the example above, the base 1000 has three noughts and so the number of digits in each complement must also be three. This is why the complement of 998 is 002 and not just 2.

Exercise 2d Multiplication with base 1000

1. 994 × 998	7. 996 × 997	13. 992 × 999	19. 979 × 999	25. 816 × 999
2. 988 × 995	8. 993 × 993	14. 993 × 997	20. 965 × 998	26. 875 × 998
3. 872 × 999	9. 995 × 993	15. 995 × 995	21. 944 × 997	27. 995 × 986
4. 896 × 997	10. 993 × 994	16. 990 × 990	22. 991 × 997	28. 993 × 976
5. 999 × 999	11. 859 × 999	17. 996 × 900	23. 988 × 996	29. 998 × 688
6. 682 × 999	12. 873 × 998	18. 989 × 989	24. 981 × 998	30. 600 × 998

Multiplication above the base

So far all the numbers we have multiplied are less than a base of 10, 100 or 1000. We can use exactly the same method to multiply numbers which are a little more than the base. An example will show how this works. Suppose we have to multiply 12 by 14.

---

1   Set the sum out as before and write the base, 10, above.

$$(10)$$
$$12$$
$$\times \underline{14}$$

2   This time the complement is a surplus because the numbers are more than 10. So we write + 2 and + 4 on the right-hand side.

$$(10)$$
$$12 + 2$$
$$\times \underline{14 + 4}$$

3   Instead of cross-subtracting we cross-add for the left-hand part of the answer. That is, 12 + 4 = 16 or 14 + 2 = 16.

$$(10)$$
$$12 + 2$$
$$\times \underline{14 + 4}$$
$$16$$

4   For the right-hand part of the answer multiply the two surplus digits 2 and 4 giving 8.

$$(10)$$
$$12 + 2$$
$$\times \underline{14 + 4}$$
$$\underline{16\ /\ 8}$$

5   The answer is 168.

Exercise 2e   Set these out as shown and answer them.

1.   11   3.   14   5.   11   7.   15   9.   11
   × 12   × 11   × 13   × 11   × 11

2.   12   4.   12   6.   12   8.   13   10.   15
   × 12   × 13   × 14   × 13   × 10

For a base of 100 there are two surplus digits for each number. The example on the next page shows this.

1	Set the sum out as before and write the base, 100, above.	(100) 112 × 1 0 4
2	The surpluses are 12 and 4. Remember that the number of digits on the right-hand side must be the same as the number of noughts in the base; in this case two.	(100) 112 + 12 × 104 + 04
3	For the left-hand part of the answer we cross-add. That is either 112 + 4 = 116, or 104 + 12 = 116.	(100) 112 + 12 × 104 + 04 116 /
4	For the right-hand part of the answer multiply the two surplus numbers, 12 and 4, giving 48.	(100) 112 + 12 × 104 + 04 116 / 48
5	The answer is 11648.	

Exercise 2f   Multiply using base 100:

1.	106 × 102	**7.**	102 × 102	**13.**	108 × 101	**19.**	106 × 101	**25.**	115 × 103
2.	102 × 109	**8.**	107 × 101	**14.**	107 × 102	**20.**	108 × 102	**26.**	120 × 104
3.	108 × 103	**9.**	103 × 102	**15.**	104 × 104	**21.**	106 × 103	**27.**	105 × 111
4.	104 × 103	**10.**	105 × 104	**16.**	105 × 110	**22.**	109 × 103	**28.**	121 × 103
5.	101 × 101	**11.**	109 × 105	**17.**	108 × 104	**23.**	112 × 104	**29.**	134 × 102
6.	102 × 101	**12.**	104 × 107	**18.**	105 × 111	**24.**	119 × 102	**30.**	198 × 101

Exercise 2g Further practice below the base 100:

1. 97 × 99	8. 95 × 91	15. 92 × 93	22. 64 × 99
2. 97 × 93	9. 93 × 95	16. 95 × 94	23. 73 × 98
3. 97 × 97	10. 88 × 93	17. 89 × 96	24. 79 × 97
4. 98 × 90	11. 91 × 93	18. 99 × 90	25. 71 × 98
5. 93 × 94	12. 90 × 92	19. 96 × 94	26. 87 × 96
6. 91 × 96	13. 95 × 88	20. 95 × 95	27. 62 × 98
7. 89 × 95	14. 76 × 99	21. 86 × 97	28. 58 × 99

Exercise 2h Further practice above the base 100:

1. 107 × 103	8. 109 × 104	15. 102 × 102	22. 103 × 103
2. 103 × 110	9. 105 × 104	16. 103 × 102	23. 108 × 102
3. 104 × 103	10. 105 × 105	17. 107 × 104	24. 108 × 112
4. 106 × 105	11. 106 × 111	18. 110 × 104	25. 122 × 103
5. 110 × 106	12. 109 × 105	19. 113 × 105	26. 135 × 102
6. 105 × 108	13. 106 × 112	20. 120 × 103	27. 147 × 101
7. 109 × 102	14. 107 × 102	21. 116 × 104	28. 118 × 102

17

Exercise 2i Revision practice

1. 99 ×97	7. 102 ×103	13. 997 ×998	19. 1002 ×1003	25. 9988 ×9998
2. 96 ×95	8. 104 ×105	14. 995 ×991	20. 1004 ×1007	26. 9675 ×9997
3. 92 ×98	9. 106 ×103	15. 994 ×995	21. 1009 ×1003	27. 9857 ×9998
4. 97 ×91	10. 107 ×108	16. 999 ×999	22. 1023 ×1002	28. 8135 ×9996
5. 76 ×97	11. 109 ×103	17. 993 ×996	23. 1012 ×1008	29. 7689 ×9998
6. 95 ×90	12. 101 ×107	18. 879 ×998	24. 1032 ×1003	30. 8799 ×9997

Exercise 2j For these mixed multiplications remember to write the correct base at the top.

1. 98 ×92	7. 92 ×97	13. 998 ×997	19. 9996 ×9998	25. 1115 ×1002
2. 99 ×97	8. 107 ×103	14. 996 ×994	20. 108 ×107	26. 97 ×88
3. 108 ×101	9. 93 ×96	15. 1004 ×1002	21. 1003 ×1009	27. 99998 ×99993
4. 95 ×95	10. 105 ×107	16. 1005 ×1008	22. 9786 ×9998	28. 635 ×999
5. 117 ×101	11. 109 ×108	17. 1008 ×1002	23. 8675 ×9997	29. 1035 ×1002
6. 132 ×102	12. 93 ×92	18. 1005 ×1010	24. 9899 ×9996	30. 99999 ×99999

Chapter Three - Division

At one there is no division. For when one is divided into six, for example, the answer is six which shows that six has not been divided at all. Division always starts at two. In the story of creation in the book of Genesis, there is division on the very first day of creation.

> *And God saw the light, that it was good:*
> *and God divided the light from the darkness.*

[Genesis 1:4]

The division into two at the beginning of creation is also the division into good and evil.

> *There are two types of created beings in this world, the Good and the Evil.*

[Bhagavad Gita 16:6]

Simple division

E.g.   4⎿1 6 4 8   a) 4 into 1 doesn't go, 4 into 16 = 4.
            4 1 2   b) 4 into 4 = 1.
                          c) 4 into 8 = 2
                          d) The answer is 412.

Exercise 3a   Division without remainders

1. 3⎿36   7. 3⎿39   13. 8⎿56   19. 3⎿9033   25. 6⎿3606

2. 2⎿84   8. 6⎿660   14. 7⎿49   20. 4⎿1648   26. 4⎿2408

3. 4⎿48   9. 4⎿448   15. 4⎿32   21. 5⎿2555   27. 3⎿2139

4. 3⎿33   10. 7⎿3577   16. 6⎿48   22. 2⎿64482   28. 2⎿1624

5. 2⎿48   11. 2⎿6824   17. 3⎿27   23. 6⎿12660   29. 4⎿2840

6. 2⎿28   12. 3⎿6399   18. 5⎿45   24. 2⎿64802   30. 5⎿1555

Division with remainders

On the other side of division we find that one cannot be divided by any number. When we try to divide one by any number the answer is always nought remainder one. For example, 5 into 1 goes 0 remainder 1, 3 into 1 goes 0 remainder 1. This just shows that whatever we try to do with the one it is always there at the end. In the same way the Absolute remains at the end of creation.

> *That is perfect., This is perfect. Perfect comes from perfect. Take perfect from perfect, the remainder is perfect.*

> [Isa Upanishad]

Exercise 3b   Division with remainders from times tables

1. 3⌊4	**7.** 3⌊16	**13.** 3⌊7	**19.** 8⌊33	**25.** 6⌊49
2. 2⌊5	**8.** 6⌊19	**14.** 4⌊3	**20.** 7⌊41	**26.** 4⌊50
3. 4⌊9	**9.** 4⌊23	**15.** 5⌊1	**21.** 4⌊38	**27.** 3⌊25
4. 3⌊10	**10.** 7⌊30	**16.** 2⌊13	**22.** 6⌊53	**28.** 2⌊23
5. 2⌊11	**11.** 2⌊21	**17.** 6⌊14	**23.** 3⌊32	**29.** 4⌊2
6. 2⌊17	**12.** 3⌊2	**18.** 2⌊1	**24.** 5⌊29	**30.** 5⌊47

The following example shows how to use remainders in the middle of a division sum. Each remainder digit is written below and to the left of the next digit.

```
4 | 2 8 6 2
  |   2   2
  -----------
    0 7 1 5 / 2
```

a) 4 into 2 goes 0 remainder 2. We do not need to write 0 at the beginning.
b) 4 into 28 goes 7.
c) 4 into 6 goes 1 remainder 2.
d) 4 into 22 goes 5 remainder 2.

Exercise 3c   Division with remainders

1. 3⌊368	7. 3⌊3223	13. 8⌊251	19. 3⌊6451	25. 6⌊1230
2. 2⌊845	8. 6⌊2469	14. 7⌊2944	20. 4⌊14234	26. 4⌊2579
3. 4⌊4833	9. 4⌊5655	15. 4⌊3539	21. 5⌊32461	27. 3⌊8790
4. 3⌊6221	10. 7⌊3526	16. 6⌊1961	22. 2⌊64532	28. 2⌊8377
5. 2⌊4887	11. 2⌊3751	17. 3⌊7241	23. 6⌊64532	29. 4⌊5247
6. 2⌊2065	12. 3⌊6728	18. 5⌊3422	24. 2⌊90910	30. 5⌊1464

Naming the parts of a division sum

A division sum has four parts which are called **divisor, dividend, quotient** and **remainder**. In the example of 4 into 2862, the divisor is 4 because it is the number we are dividing by. 2862 is called the dividend and is the number that is being divided. 715 is called the quotient, which is the result of the division. 2 is the remainder because it is that which remains.

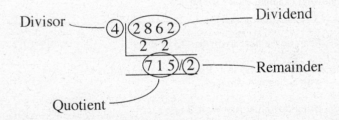

The following rhyme will help you to remember the parts of a division sum:-

The divisor is the number that divides the dividend, the answer is the quotient, the remainder's at the end.

Dividing by Nine

The following method for dividing by nine is really a special case of Nikhilam division. To begin with we will look at some very easy examples of division by nine.

In these examples, each number to be divided has been separated into two parts by a diagonal stroke. You will notice that the left-hand part gives the first part of the answer and the two parts added together gives the remainder. For 9 into 12, for example, the first digit of 12, that is 1, is the first part of the answer, and the two digits of 12 added together, that is $1 + 2 = 3$, gives the remainder.

$$9\lfloor 1/0 \qquad 9\lfloor 1/2 \qquad 9\lfloor 2/1 \qquad 9\lfloor 3/3$$
$$\quad 1/1 \qquad\qquad 1/3 \qquad\qquad 2/3 \qquad\qquad 3/6$$

$$9\lfloor 4/0 \qquad 9\lfloor 5/2 \qquad 9\lfloor 6/1 \qquad 9\lfloor 7/0$$
$$\quad 4/4 \qquad\qquad 5/7 \qquad\qquad 6/7 \qquad\qquad 7/7$$

We can use this fact to divide bigger numbers by nine. Having written down the first digit of the answer, which is the same as the first digit of the dividend, each answer digit is found simply by adding the last quotient digit to the next dividend digit.

The following example shows the method:

---

a) Suppose we have to divide 113 by nine. $\qquad 9\lfloor 1\,1\,/\,3$

b) Separate off the last digit of the dividend, 113, with a diagonal stroke.

c) Bring down the first digit, 1.

d) Add this to the next dividend digit, $1 + 1 = 2$ $\qquad 9\lfloor 1\,1\,/\,3$
and put this down as the next digit of the quotient. $\qquad\qquad\underline{\quad 1\,2\,/\,5}$

e) Add this to the next digit of the dividend, $2 + 3 = 5$, and this gives the remainder.

f) The answer is 12 remainder 5.

Exercise 3d   Dividing by nine

1. 9⌊111	**7.** 9⌊123	**13.** 9⌊412	**19.** 9⌊1121	**25.** 9⌊11102
2. 9⌊121	**8.** 9⌊107	**14.** 9⌊503	**20.** 9⌊1241	**26.** 9⌊12211
3. 9⌊142	**9.** 9⌊143	**15.** 9⌊620	**21.** 9⌊2111	**27.** 9⌊42110
4. 9⌊122	**10.** 9⌊201	**16.** 9⌊611	**22.** 9⌊3121	**28.** 9⌊12031
5. 9⌊150	**11.** 9⌊211	**17.** 9⌊232	**23.** 9⌊3210	**29.** 9⌊20321
6. 9⌊103	**12.** 9⌊321	**18.** 9⌊520	**24.** 9⌊4102	**30.** 9⌊80000

Nikhilam division

We first take up the case of dividing a number by a single digit divisor which is near to 10, starting with 8.

Suppose we want to divide 8 into 111.

a) Set the sum out as before but this time write the complement of 8, that is 2, underneath the 8.

$$\begin{array}{c|c} 8 & 1\ 1\ /\ 1 \\ 2 & \\ \hline \end{array}$$

b) The complement 2 is to become a multiplier.

c) Bring down the first digit, 1. Multiply this 1 by the complement, that is $1 \times 2 = 2$, and write this underneath the next dividend digit.

$$\begin{array}{c|c} 8 & 1\ 1\ /\ 1 \\ 2 & \ \ 2 \\ \hline & 1 \end{array}$$

d) Add up the second column, $1 + 2 = 3$, and this is the next quotient digit.

$$\begin{array}{c|c} 8 & 1\ 1\ /\ 1 \\ 2 & \ \ 2 \\ \hline & 1\ 3 \end{array}$$

e) Multiply this 3 by the complement, that is $3 \times 2 = 6$, and place the 6 under the last 1.

$$\begin{array}{c|c} 8 & 1\ 1\ /\ 1 \\ 2 & \ \ 2\ \ 6 \\ \hline & 1\ 3\ /\ 7 \end{array}$$

f) Add up the final column for the remainder, $1 + 6 = 7$.

g) The answer is 13 remainder 7.

Exercise 3e   Use Nikhilam division.

1. 8⌐22	**5.** 7⌐13	**9.** 9⌐40	**13.** 9⌐42	**17.** 9⌐2401
2. 8⌐31	**6.** 7⌐20	**10.** 9⌐33	**14.** 9⌐31	**18.** 9⌐4000
3. 8⌐101	**7.** 9⌐21	**11.** 8⌐23	**15.** 9⌐100	**19.** 9⌐2330
4. 8⌐102	**8.** 9⌐24	**12.** 9⌐61	**16.** 9⌐1401	**20.** 9⌐18

Divisors with base 100 and 1000

With a base of 100 we use the complement of the divisor and leave two digits for the remainder portion. The following example shows how this is done.

In this example we have to divide 88 into 123.

$$88 | 1 / 2\ 3$$
$$12 |$$
$$1$$

a) The sum is set out as shown with the complement of 88, that is 12, written underneath.

b) Since the base of the divisor is 100, we leave two digits on the right of the remainder stroke. The first digit, 1, is brought down as before.

$$88 | 1 / 2\ 3$$
$$12 |\quad 1\ 2$$
$$1$$

c) We next multiply this 1 by the complement, $1 \times 12 = 12$, and write these two digits under the next two numbers in the dividend.

$$88 | 1 / 2\ 3$$
$$12 |\quad 1\ 2$$

d) Finally, add up for the remainder, 35, and the answer is 1 remainder 35.

$$1 / 3\ 5$$

Exercise 3f   Nikhilam division

1. 88⌐113	**5.** 85⌐155	**9.** 73⌐126	**13.** 68⌐104	**17.** 78⌐210
2. 86⌐124	**6.** 96⌐201	**10.** 91⌐264	**14.** 99⌐536	**18.** 94⌐319
3. 78⌐108	**7.** 97⌐234	**11.** 87⌐165	**15.** 77⌐122	**19.** 85⌐250
4. 79⌐142	**8.** 93⌐126	**12.** 93⌐204	**16.** 98⌐613	**20.** 82⌐166

Exercise 3g

1. $78 \lfloor 147$ 5. $95 \lfloor 342$ 9. $78 \lfloor 311$ 13. $82 \lfloor 147$ 17. $94 \lfloor 366$

2. $58 \lfloor 115$ 6. $76 \lfloor 221$ 10. $86 \lfloor 240$ 14. $75 \lfloor 222$ 18. $87 \lfloor 258$

3. $89 \lfloor 246$ 7. $93 \lfloor 422$ 11. $99 \lfloor 784$ 15. $96 \lfloor 478$ 19. $84 \lfloor 251$

4. $82 \lfloor 201$ 8. $85 \lfloor 233$ 12. $88 \lfloor 334$ 16. $92 \lfloor 212$ 20. $89 \lfloor 439$

Nikhilam division with any base

The next stage is to divide with any large divisor close to a base. It is important to remember the base because the number of noughts in the base gives the number of digits which must be left after the remainder stroke. So for a base of 10 we leave one digit after the remainder stroke, for a base of 100 two digits must be left, and for a base of 1000, three digits must be left.
The following rhyme helps to remember the rule about remainder digits:-

> **For the number of digits on the right,**
> **keep the noughts of the base in sight.**

Divide 1374 by 878

a) The number of digits in the base, 1000, is the same as the number of digits in the remainder and so the remainder stroke is placed between 1 and 3.

$$8\ 7\ 8 | 1\ /\ 3\ 7\ 4$$

b) The complement of 878, found by *All from nine and the last from ten*, is 122 and is written below the divisor.

$$8\ 7\ 8 | 1\ /\ 3\ 7\ 4$$
$$1\ 2\ 2$$
$$1$$

c) The first quotient digit, 1, is brought straight down into the answer.

d) $1 \times 122 = 122$, and this is placed below 374 with the digits in line.

$$8\ 7\ 8 | 1\ /\ 3\ 7\ 4$$
$$1\ 2\ 2 | \qquad 1\ 2\ 2$$
$$1\ /\ 4\ 9\ 6$$

e) $374 + 122$ gives the remainder and so the answer is 1 remainder 496.

Exercise 3h Using different bases

1. 88 | 121

2. 76 | 111

3. 83 | 132

4. 79 | 107

5. 83 | 144

6. 73 | 129

7. 779 | 1111

8. 866 | 1234

9. 8877 | 12034

10. 8907 | 13103

11. 7999 | 12131

12. 790 | 1212

13. 887 | 1223

14. 893 | 1555

15. 828 | 1133

16. 867 | 1313

17. 93 | 121

18. 987 | 1248

Exercise 3i Further practice with different bases

1. 88 | 224

2. 89 | 306

3. 76 | 143

4. 84 | 233

5. 98 | 103

6. 97 | 104

7. 995 | 1170

8. 991 | 2415

9. 9987 | 22122

10. 9879 | 12312

11. 9807 | 12432

12. 999 | 3786

13. 989 | 4121

14. 789 | 1543

15. 799 | 1444

16. 687 | 1022

17. 901 | 1143

18. 786 | 1222

Chapter Four - Digital Roots

Adding the digits of a number

If we add up the digits of a number until there is only one number left we have found what is called the digital root.

For 5674, $5 + 6 + 7 + 4 = 22$, and $2 + 2 = 4$.

4 is the digital root of 5674.

Exercise 4a Write down the digital root of:

1. 23	11. 39	21. 123	31. 1332
2. 26	12. 95	22. 245	32. 4231
3. 12	13. 87	23. 635	33. 4621
4. 35	14. 68	24. 409	34. 5103
5. 42	15. 59	25. 881	35. 35210
6. 61	16. 77	26. 672	36. 20000
7. 72	17. 86	27. 594	37. 216102
8. 44	18. 93	28. 911	38. 912432
9. 24	19. 37	29. 638	39. 210032
10. 11	20. 64	30. 256	40. 999999

The digital root of a number is also the remainder we find when that number is divided by nine.

For example, 9 into 12 goes 1 remainder 3, The remainder is 3 and the digital root of 12 is 3. Again, 9 into 32 goes 3 remainder 5, and the digital root of 32 is 5.

Digital roots for the times tables

We are now going to look at the digital roots of the answers to the times tables. These give interesting number patterns. We will start with the **4×** table.

We can write down the answers to the four times table and for every answer which is more than 9, add up the digits to find the digital root.

							DIGITAL ROOT
1 × 4 = 4							4
2 × 4 = 8							8
3 × 4 = 12	1 + 2 = 3						3
4 × 4 = 16	1 + 6 = 7						7
5 × 4 = 20	2 + 0 = 2						2
6 × 4 = 24	2 + 4 = 6						6
7 × 4 = 28	2 + 8 = 10	1 + 0 = 1		1
8 × 4 = 32	3 + 2 = 5						5
9 × 4 = 36	3 + 6 = 9						9
10 × 4 = 40	4 + 0 = 4						4
11 × 4 = 44	4 + 4 = 8						8
12 × 4 = 48	4 + 8 = 12	1 + 2 = 3		3

The pattern of digital roots is, 4, 8, 3, 7, 2, 6, 1, 5, 9.

After this the pattern repeats itself and will carry on repeating itself if we continue the table on for higher numbers.

To see the pattern in these numbers we will plot them on the circle of nine points. To do this, start at 4 and draw a straight line from 4 to 8. Then draw a straight line from 8 to 3, the next number. In the same way draw lines from 3 to 7, 7 to 2, 2 to 6, 1 to 5, 5 to 9 and 9 to 4.

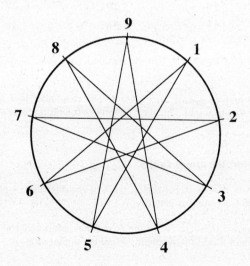

WORK SHEET FOR DIGITAL ROOTS OF TIMES TABLES

Exercise 4b Find the digital root patterns for the 2×, 3×, 5×, 6×, 7×, and 8× tables. Which patterns are the same?

DIGITAL
ROOT

1 ×	=		+	=		+	=	
2 ×	=		+	=		+	=	
3 ×	=		+	=		+	=	
4 ×	=		+	=		+	=	
5 ×	=		+	=		+	=	
6 ×	=		+	=		+	=	
7 ×	=		+	=		+	=	
8 ×	=		+	=		+	=	
9 ×	=		+	=		+	=	
10 ×	=		+	=		+	=	
11 ×	=		+	=		+	=	
12 ×	=		+	=		+	=	

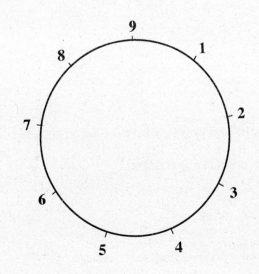

29

Casting Out Nines

An easy way of finding the digital root of a large number is to cast out nines. This is done by crossing out any nines in the number or any digits adding up to nine. The numbers which are left at the end are added up for the digital root. Look at the following example. The sutra used here is *By Elimination and Retention*..

Example: Find the digital root of 19462785.

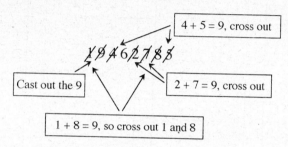

The only number which is left is 6 and this is the digital root.

Example: Find the digital root of 257520643.

$$2\,5\,7\,5\,2\,0\,3\,4\,3$$

Steps:

1. 2 + 7 = 9, cross out 2 and 7.
2. 4 + 3 + 2 = 9, cross out 4, 3 and 2.
3. There are no other groups of numbers adding up to 9.
4. Add up the remaining digits, 5 + 5 + 0 + 3 = 13.
5. 13 is more than 9, so 1 + 3 = 4.
6. The digital root is 4.

If there is nothing left after having cast out nines then the digital root is 9.

Example: Find the digital root of 432362781

Steps:

1. 4 + 3 + 2 = 9, cast out.
2. 3 + 6 = 9, cast out.
3. 2 + 7 = 9, cast out.
4. 8 + 1 = 9, cast out.
5. There is nothing left and so 9 is the digital root.

Exercise 4c Write down the following numbers and find the digital root by casting out nines:

1. 813	11. 647322	21. 897364	31. 367425
2. 366	12. 432701	22. 230098	32. 538987
3. 574	13. 946534	23. 876221	33. 182799
4. 722	14. 357096	24. 994652	34. 678321
5. 75002	15. 123789	25. 65743	35. 354621
6. 34625	16. 362811	26. 94804	36. 768511
7. 162307	17. 43432	27. 125789	37. 473821
8. 44565	18. 9798	28. 657483	38. 98076
9. 87612	19. 43985	29. 832762	39. 812763
10. 32366	20. 99876	30. 999987	40. 978132

The 9× Table

Here is the 9× table with its digital roots.

			9
1 × 9 = 9			9
2 × 9 = 18	1 + 8 9		9
3 × 9 = 27	2 + 7 = 9		9
4 × 9 = 36	3 + 6 = 9		9
5 × 9 = 45	4 + 5 = 9		9
6 × 9 = 54	5 + 4 = 9		9
7 × 9 = 63	6 + 3 = 9		9
8 × 9 = 72	7 + 2 = 9		9
9 × 9 = 81	8 + 1 = 9		9
10 × 9 = 90	9 + 0 = 9		9
11 × 9 = 99	9 + 9 = 18	1 + 8 = 9	9
12 × 9 = 108	1 + 8 = 9		9

The digital roots are all nine! This is because nine is the perfect number, it can never be broken. Whatever nine is multiplied by it always comes to nine. This also works for division. If a number has a digital root of nine then it is exactly divisible by nine.

Chapter Five - Multiplication by Vertically and Crosswise

In chapter two on Nikhilam multiplication, all the multiplication sums had at least one of the numbers to be multiplied close to a particular base of 10, 100, 1000, etc. The Nikhilam method is a special case formula. We now proceed to deal with the general formula which may be used for all cases of multiplication. The Vedic sutra for this is, *Urdhva Tiryagbhyam* and which means,

Vertically and Crosswise.

There are many applications of this short sutra and a simple example will show how it works in practice.

Suppose we have to multiply 42 by 13.

a) Starting at the left, multiply the two left-hand most digits, *vertically*, that is, $4 \times 1 = 4$, and set the answer down underneath as the left-hand most part of the answer.

$$\begin{array}{r} 4\ \ 2 \\ \times\ 1\ \ 3 \\ \hline 4 \end{array}$$

b) We then multiply 4 by 3 and 2 by 1, *crosswise*, and add these two answers together, $4 \times 3 = 12$ and $2 \times 1 = 2$, and $12 + 2 = 14$. Set down the 4 as the next answer digit and carry the 1 to the left.

$$\begin{array}{r} 4\ \ 2 \\ 1\ \ 3 \\ \times\ 4\ \ 4 \\ 1 \end{array}$$

c) We multiply 2 by 3, *vertically*, and set down the answer, 6, as the right-hand most answer digit.

d) Add in the carry digit to give the answer 546.

$$\begin{array}{r} 4\ \ 2 \\ 1\ \ 3 \\ \times\ 4\ \ 4\ \ 6 \\ 1 \\ \hline 5\ \ 4\ \ 6 \end{array}$$

N.B. This method can be started either from the right or from the left.

Exercise 5a   Use Vertically and Crosswise to multiply the following:

1.	31 × 12	3.	12 × 13	5.	32 × 13	7.	20 × 21
2.	21 × 11	4.	22 × 14	6.	14 × 11	8.	23 × 30

9.	11 × <u>12</u>	**17.**	35 × <u>12</u>	**25.**	14 × <u>39</u>	**33.**	38 × <u>32</u>
10.	12 × <u>12</u>	**18.**	24 × <u>13</u>	**26.**	49 × <u>15</u>	**34.**	42 × <u>39</u>
11.	21 × <u>23</u>	**19.**	76 × <u>11</u>	**27.**	16 × <u>53</u>	**35.**	71 × <u>53</u>
12.	16 × <u>13</u>	**20.**	35 × <u>22</u>	**28.**	12 × <u>48</u>	**36.**	84 × <u>67</u>
13.	19 × <u>13</u>	**21.**	26 × <u>14</u>	**29.**	59 × <u>17</u>	**37.**	91 × <u>75</u>
14.	27 × <u>14</u>	**22.**	34 × <u>14</u>	**30.**	42 × <u>15</u>	**38.**	10 × <u>11</u>
15.	16 × <u>32</u>	**23.**	41 × <u>51</u>	**31.**	23 × <u>23</u>	**39.**	34 × <u>11</u>
16.	13 × <u>21</u>	**24.**	15 × <u>45</u>	**32.**	56 × <u>26</u>	**40.**	26 × <u>11</u>

When two numbers are multiplied together the answer is called the **product**.
For 2 × 3 = 6, the answer 6 is the product of 2 and 3.

Find the cost of 23 pencils at 72p each.

Set the numbers out so that they can be multiplied.

```
      23
   ×  72
    1456
       2
    1656
```

a) 2 × 7 = 14
b) 2 × 2 + 7 × 3 = 25
c) 3 × 2 = 6

Cost is   £16.56

So 23 times 72 pence is found to be 1656 pence.
The answer is then converted into pounds by dividing
1656p by 100. The answer is then £16.56

33

Exercise 5b Problems: each sum should be set out for vertically and crosswise.

1. Multiply 46 by 32.

2. Find the product of 23 and 48.

3. What is 53 times 84?

4. Multiply forty-two by twenty-eight.

5. Find the cost of sixteen radios at £53 each.

6. If there are 17 girls in a class and each one has 14 crayons, how many crayons are there altogether.

7. What is twenty-four lots of 12?

8. Find the product of thirty-eight and sixteen.

9. A coach company has 21 coaches and each coach can carry 53 passengers. How many passengers can all the coaches carry?

10. A block of stamps has 24 rows with 14 in each row How many stamps are there in the block?

11. If a packet of biscuits costs 64p, find the cost of a whole box containing forty-eight packets.

12. Find the cost of 28 metres of dress fabric if one metre costs £34.

13. A car-park can fit 35 rows of cars with 51 in each row. Find the number of cars that can fit into the car-park.

14. Calculate the number of hours in the month of January.

15. 24 folders each have fifty-six sheets of paper inside them. How many sheets of paper are there altogether?

16. An army had thirty-eight armoured personel carriers. If each vehicle carries twelve soldiers, how many soldiers can all the carriers take?

17. A girl learnt 20 verses of scripture a day for each of 48 days. How many verses did she learn in that time?

18. If you can do twenty-five sums a day, how many sums can you do in fourteen days?

Multiplying by a single digit

Multiplying by a single digit is really just a special case of vertically and crosswise.

Example   234
        ×   4
         936
         11

a) 4 × 4 = 16, put down the 6 and carry 1.
b) 4 × 3 = 12, add the carry 1, which makes 13, put down the 3 and carry 1.
c) 4 × 2 = 8, add the carry 1, making 9.
d) The answer is 936.

Exercise 5c Multiply:

1. 24 × 2	11. 123 × 2	21. 3241 × 2	31. 10023 × 2
2. 32 × 2	12. 403 × 2	22. 3210 × 5	32. 24319 × 2
3. 44 × 2	13. 512 × 3	23. 2441 × 3	33. 20341 × 3
4. 25 × 3	14. 111 × 6	24. 1023 × 4	34. 32012 × 5
5. 41 × 3	15. 323 × 2	25. 6022 × 3	35. 51102 × 6
6. 21 × 4	16. 420 × 1	26. 4510 × 6	36. 23415 × 8
7. 31 × 3	17. 300 × 3	27. 2739 × 2	37. 64531 × 9
8. 34 × 2	18. 541 × 2	28. 6712 × 3	38. 43243 × 7
9. 24 × 3	19. 104 × 4	29. 7982 × 2	39. 65741 × 8
10. 26 × 2	20. 340 × 3	30. 1089 × 4	40. 87656 × 9

Exercise 5d Multiply:

1.	201014 × 2	**4.**	461103 × 2	**7.**	140551 × 4	**10.**	4352231 × 8
2.	113232 × 2	**5.**	113403 × 4	**8.**	115360 × 6	**11.**	123456 × 9
3.	4001514 × 3	**6.**	523012 × 5	**9.**	938541 × 3	**12.**	142857 × 7

Multiplying larger numbers

The Vertically and Crosswise method may easily be extended to multiplying numbers containing any number of digits but for now we take up the case of multiplying two three-digit numbers.

Multiply 362 by 134

$$\begin{array}{r} 362 \\ \times\ 134 \\ \hline 3 \end{array}$$

a) Starting from the left, the first answer digit is
$3 \times 1 = 3$.

$$\begin{array}{r} 362 \\ \times\ 134 \\ \hline 35 \\ 1 \end{array}$$

b) The next answer digit is the sum of the cross-product of the four left-hand most digits, that is,
$(3 \times 3) + (6 \times 1) = 15$.

$$\begin{array}{r} 362 \\ \times\ 134 \\ \hline 352 \\ 13 \end{array}$$

c) The middle step is to add the cross-product of all six digits in the following order,
$(3 \times 4) + (6 \times 3) + (2 \times 1) = 32$.

$$\begin{array}{r} 362 \\ \times\ 134 \\ \hline 3520 \\ 133 \end{array}$$

d) The sum of the cross-product of the four right-hand most digits gives the next answer digit, that is
$(6 \times 4) + (2 \times 3) = 30$.

$$\begin{array}{r} 362 \\ \times\ 134 \\ \hline 35208 \\ 133 \end{array}$$

e) The final step is the product of the two right-hand most digits, $2 \times 4 = 8$.

f) After adding up the carry digits the answer is found to be 48508.

$$\begin{array}{r} 35208 \\ 133 \\ \hline 48508 \end{array}$$

The diagram below may help remember the vertically and crosswise pattern required for multiplying two three-digit numbers together. Each dot represents a digit in the number and the lines joining the dots stand for digits to be multiplied.

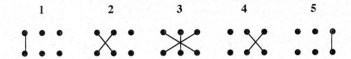

| 1 | 2 | 3 | 4 | 5 |

Exercise 5e* Find the following products: if the number has only two digits then you may fill the empty hundreds column with a nought.

1. 123 × 121	**11.** 412 × 312	**21.** 312 × 212
2. 144 × 162	**12.** 423 × 203	**22.** 203 × 133
3. 127 × 354	**13.** 270 × 131	**23.** 364 × 623
4. 309 × 341	**14.** 400 × 413	**24.** 789 × 121
5. 477 × 121	**15.** 512 × 370	**25.** 117 × 203
6. 147 × 231	**16.** 208 × 51	**26.** 909 × 131
7. 143 × 641	**17.** 421 × 48	**27.** 353 × 522
8. 402 × 375	**18.** 35 × 374	**28.** 516 × 733
9. 523 × 423	**19.** 318 × 25	**29.** 777 × 120
10. 415 × 634	**20.** 78 × 324	**30.** 45 × 433

Exercise 5f* Problems

1. Find the product of 135 and 216.

2. Multiply one hundred and two by 640.

3. There are 505 matches in a large box and a carton contains 124 such boxes. Find the number of matches in a carton.

4. A bookshop sells 563 copies of a book at £7.25 per book. How much was taken for the sale of the books?

5. Find the result of multiplying 387 by 24.

6. A fruit-picker can harvest 56 boxes of strawberries in one hour. If she works for 126 hours over a three week period, how many boxes does she fill?

7. In one evening a cinema sells 346 tickets at £3.25 each. How much is received for the sale of these tickets?

8. Find the cost of 144 eggs at 15p each.

9. A man pays £364 per month for a mortgage. Find how much he will have paid over a period of 25 years.

10. If 12 Norwegian kroner are worth £1, how many kroners would you expect for £250?

11. Lettuces are packed 35 to a crate. How many lettuces are there in 300 crates?

12. What is the result of 101 multiplied by 101?

13. How many square metres of turf will be needed to make a lawn 27 metres wide and 132 metres long?

14. A factory used 468 tons of coal at £113 per ton. What was the cost of all the coal?

15. A group of 158 pupils and 4 adults go to an exhibition for which the entry fee is 25p for children and 50p for adults. For how much must a cheque be made out for the whole party?

Exercise 5g There is no carrying to be done with these. Write answers only.

1.	24 × 12	5.	12 × 22	9.	41 × 12	13.	221 × 220
2.	22 × 13	6.	40 × 32	10.	15 × 11	14.	401 × 201
3.	44 × 11	7.	51 × 21	11.	32 × 20	15.	303 × 112
4.	21 × 13	8.	31 × 31	12.	30 × 20	16.	101 × 122

Chapter Six - Subtraction by Nikhilam

Complements

In this chapter, the Nikhilam rule is used for subtraction. We have already seen how the complement of a number is obtained by using the All from nine and the last from ten rule and relates any number back to unity The following examples and exercise are given as reminders.

To find the complement of 3648,
a) 3 from 9 = 6   3648
b) 6 from 9 = 3   6352
c) 4 from 9 = 5
d) 8 (the last) from 10 = 2
The complement is 6352.

To find the complement of 30400,
a) 3 from 9 = 6   30400
b) 0 from 9 = 9   69600
c) 4 (the last number) from 10 = 6
d) Any final noughts are brought straight down.
The complement is 69600

Exercise 6a Find the complements of the following:

1.	86	11.	3205	21.	43004
2.	58	12.	8967	22.	623000
3.	842	13.	4300	23.	7000
4.	341	14.	5007	24.	12000
5.	720	15.	9001	25.	7890
6.	672	16.	70101	26.	64040
7.	666	17.	103004	27.	980030
8.	846	18.	436	28.	43007010
9.	840	19.	97	29.	68081001
10.	899	20.	500017	30.	4000500

Subtraction using complements

In the simple case, such as 365 – 215, when the sum is set out we find that all of the top row digits are greater than or equal to the digits directly below. In this example, each digit is subtracted from the one above.

$$
\begin{array}{r}
365 \\
-\ 215 \\
\hline
150
\end{array}
$$

Complements are used when this is not the case. The basic method is to take the difference of the two digits and, when the bottom row digit is larger, write down the complement of the difference. When complements are no longer needed we subtract an extra 1 from the next left-hand column. To see how this works in practice follow the steps in the example below.

Subtract 3876 from 5322.

a) Starting from the right, 6 is more than 2, so we take the difference, 4, and write down its complement from 10 (since it is the last), that is, 6.

$$
\begin{array}{r}
5322 \\
-\ 3876 \\
\hline
6
\end{array}
$$

b) In the next column, the difference between 7 and 2 is 5 and the complement (from 9) is 4.

$$
\begin{array}{r}
5322 \\
-\ 3876 \\
\hline
46
\end{array}
$$

c) For the hundreds column, the difference between 8 and 3 is 5 and the complement of this is 4.

$$
\begin{array}{r}
5322 \\
-\ 3876 \\
\hline
446
\end{array}
$$

d) In the thousands column, 5 is greater than 3 and so we can finish using complements. This is done by reducing the answer by 1 after the ordinary subtraction, that is, 5 – 3 – 1 = 1.

$$
\begin{array}{r}
5322 \\
-\ 3876 \\
\hline
1446
\end{array}
$$

e) The answer is 1446.

Exercise 6b

1.   4121
   – 2787
	6. 7231
	   – 6452
		11. 34121
		    – 15678
			16. 42374
			    – 7485

2.   5432
   – 1567
	7. 8191
	   – 6292
		12. 35133
		    – 16249
			17. 53611
			    – 7899

3.   6000
   – 4872
	8. 4242
	   – 1353
		13. 27000
		    – 18123
			18. 48764
			    – 19976

4.   5132
   – 1763
	9. 5612
	   – 1777
		14. 57988
		    – 18999
			19. 13478
			    – 9589

5.   3221
   – 1762
	10. 4111
	   – 1444
		15. 10000
		    – 6987
			20. 62488
			    – 3489

Starting with complements in the middle of a sum

To start using complements at any point in the subtraction treat the particular column as if it was the first on the right.

Subtract 19670 from 56381

a) In the first two columns on the right, the digits in the top row are greater than those below. $1 - 0 = 1$, $8 - 7 = 1$.

$$\begin{array}{r} 56381 \\ -19670 \\ \hline 11 \end{array}$$

b) In the hundreds column, 6 is greater than 3 and so we start using complements here. Difference is 3, complement (from 10) is 7.

$$\begin{array}{r} 56381 \\ -19670 \\ \hline 711 \end{array}$$

c) In the next column, the difference 3, the complement (from 9) is 6.

$$\begin{array}{r} 56381 \\ -19670 \\ \hline 6711 \end{array}$$

d) For the last step, where 5 is greater than 1, we take an extra 1 off to finish using complements, $5 - 1 - 1 = 3$.

$$\begin{array}{r} 56381 \\ -19670 \\ \hline 36711 \end{array}$$

Exercise 6c

1.	4327 – 1515	**6.**	8241 – 4341	**11.**	32467 – 14533	**16.**	76589 – 16688
2.	3672 – 1981	**7.**	643 – 171	**12.**	76019 – 29128	**17.**	43723 – 19780
3.	4849 – 2954	**8.**	9730 – 1820	**13.**	32456 – 14321	**18.**	32346 – 18223
4.	3760 – 1910	**9.**	7578 – 2921	**14.**	66220 – 49110	**19.**	76542 – 17691
5.	7328 – 1631	**10.**	13147 – 9453	**15.**	43720 – 9810	**20.**	64321 – 15430

Finishing with complements in the middle of a sum

The procedure for finishing with complements at any particular column in a subtraction requires that the digit in the top row is greater than the digit directly below. The process is to subtract and then take 1 off.

Subtract 3459 from 6753

a) In the units column, the difference is 6, and the complement is 4.

$$\begin{array}{r} 6753 \\ -\ 3459 \\ \hline 4 \end{array}$$

b) In the tens column, 5 is not greater than 5 and so we stay with the complements. Difference is 0, complement, 9.

$$\begin{array}{r} 6753 \\ -\ 3459 \\ \hline 94 \end{array}$$

c) 7 is greater than 4, so 7 – 4 – 1 = 2.

$$\begin{array}{r} 6753 \\ -\ 3459 \\ \hline 294 \end{array}$$

d) In the left hand column, 6 – 3 = 3.

e) The answer is 3294.

$$\begin{array}{r} 6753 \\ -\ 3459 \\ \hline 3294 \end{array}$$

Exercise 6d

1.	5713 – 1246	**9.**	468 – 129	**17.**	32400 – 11378	**25.**	47823 – 25365
2.	2311 – 1179	**10.**	334 – 215	**18.**	46000 – 12187	**26.**	54262 – 11373
3.	6234 – 1078	**11.**	7811 – 4622	**19.**	32544 – 12359	**27.**	63974 – 22887
4.	7843 – 1237	**12.**	3817 – 1968	**20.**	67813 – 64404	**28.**	72381 – 31296
5.	6894 – 3726	**13.**	7318 – 5109	**21.**	79308 – 45219	**29.**	84623 – 53164
6.	7564 – 1299	**14.**	6453 – 1239	**22.**	53462 – 12678	**30.**	12345 – 11999
7.	3546 – 1378	**15.**	7013 – 3008	**23.**	60981 – 20895	**31.**	50256 – 20178
8.	2354 – 1068	**16.**	5453 – 1239	**24.**	46875 – 12999	**32**	76512 – 12634

The general case of subtraction

The general case is where complements are only used when necessary in a subtraction.sum There are four points to remember with Nikhilam subtraction:

1) Go into complements when the digit in the bottom row is larger than the one above.

2) The first complement is from ten and the rest are from nine.

3) Come out of complements when the digit in the top row is larger than the one below.

4) When coming out of complements drop 1 in that column.

The example on the next page shows how to start and finish using complements more than once in a single subtraction.

671245 − 380674

$\qquad$
671245
− 380674
——————
1

a) 5 − 4 = 1

671245
− 380674
——————
71

b) Difference 3, complement 7.

671245
− 380674
——————
571

c) Difference 4, complement 5.

671245
− 380674
——————
0571

d) 1 − 0 − 1 = 0

671245
− 380674
——————
90571

e) Difference 1, complement 9.

671245
− 380674
——————
90571

f) 6 − 3 − 1 = 2

671245
− 380674
——————
290571

g) The answer is 290571.

Exercise 6e

1. 54326 − 12784	6. 765432 − 345678	11. 846123 − 728321	16. 363239 − 177190
2. 71209 − 34326	7. 326542 − 123456	12. 723068 − 91129	17. 217829 − 9183
3. 64156 − 2374	8. 36271 − 2123	13. 432157 − 81623	18. 462142 − 191806
4. 835421 − 642561	9. 100000 − 76543	14. 534087 − 80089	19. 361526 − 45619
5. 945632 − 456789	10. 932640 − 175294	15. 145629 − 8917	20. 948134 − 419918

The word *minus* means subtract or take away and comes from the Latin word meaning *less*.

Exercise 6f Problems

1. Find the difference between £763 and £489.

2. Subtract 23478 from 56712.

3. What is 6050 minus 489?

4. Subtract £23000 from £52500.

5. Find the difference between the heights of William and Jessica if William is 167 cm tall and Jessica is 129 cm tall.

6. A builder has a pile of 1200 bricks. If he uses 956 of them to build a wall, how many are left unused?

7. A furniture store has 2154 pieces of furniture for sale. If 1951 are unsold at the end of a month, how many have been sold during that month?

8. A man has £2923 in a savings account and spends £1635 on having a garage built. How much does he have left?

9. A theatre has a seating capacity of eight hundred. On one evening there were one hundred and sixty four spare seats. How many people were in the audience that night?

10. A newspaper shop had 3564 newspapers for sale in a week. How many were sold if there were 780 left at the end of the week?

11. In a town in Peru there were 1230 homes. An earthquake destroyed 851 of these homes. How many were left?

12. A man owes the bank £680. Find his remaining debt when he pays back £495 of the outstanding amount.

13. A farmer has 3025 lambs and sells 896 of them at the sheep market. How many does he have after the sale?

14. A book has 198 pages. If I have read 69 of them, how many pages do I have left to read?

15. A man bought set of screw-drivers which cost £7.42. How much change should he receive from a twenty pound note?

45

Chapter Seven - Vulgar Fractions

What is a fraction?

One is Absolute, and this Absolute is the innermost Self of us all. Everything comes from One and without it nothing could be made which is made. Since One is Absolute, it is unchanging - forever the same. As such it can not be divided. The number one is indivisible.

In the creation we pretend that the One can be divided. We pretend that it can be divided into two, three, four, and so on. This is done through name. We should always remember that One cannot be divided, that we only pretend that it can be. Of course, if we forget that it is indivisible then its divisions become real and true.

Think of an apple. It is a whole, a one. Now think of it as cut into two pieces. Each piece is now a One and so the unity has not been lost. The appearance is of two halves but in fact there is one whole apple and each half is itself a whole piece.

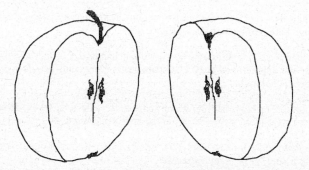

In mathematics we can say that each piece of apple is 'one divided by two'. This is why a half is written as $\frac{1}{2}$. The line in between the 1 and the 2 means divide. But because we cannot really divide one by two we have to write $\frac{1}{2}$ as an incomplete division sum. When we pretend that it is a finished division then we have the idea of one half.

Similarly, when we try to divide one by three we arrive at one third which is written as $\frac{1}{3}$. Again one divided by four is a quarter or one fourth, which is written as $\frac{1}{4}$.

Here is a diagram of a disc cut into three equal pieces. Each piece is a third of the whole.

One third is written as $\frac{1}{3}$. The one on top tells us that one whole is being divided and the three on the bottom tells us that the one is divided into three pieces. $\frac{1}{3}$ also tells us that of thirds we have one of them and not two, which is written as $\frac{2}{3}$, or any other number of thirds.

A vulgar fraction has a number on top and a number on the bottom with a line between the two numbers. The other sort of fraction is a decimal fraction which has a decimal point. The word vulgar means 'rude' or 'unfinished' and since this type of fraction is an unfinished division it is called vulgar.

Exercise 7a Write the following fractions in figures:

1. one fifth	11. one tenth	21. five sevenths
2. one seventh	12. four fifths	22. nine thirteenths
3. two thirds	13. five sixths	23. six elevenths
4. three quarters	14. four ninths	24. eight fifteenths
5. three fifths	15. three eigths	25. ten seventeenths
6. one sixth	16. one twentieth	26. thirteen twentieths
7. two ninths	17. three twelfths	27. seven nineteenths
8. three sevenths	18. six elevenths	28. four fifteenths
9. nine tenths	19. two fifteenths	29. three fiftieths
10. seven twelfths	20. seven eigths	30. seventeen hundredths

Denominator

The number on the bottom of a fraction is called the **denominator**. It tells us how many parts the whole is divided into.

Here is a list of names of some denominators:

$\frac{?}{2}$ halves	$\frac{?}{12}$ twelfths	$\frac{?}{22}$ twenty-seconds
$\frac{?}{3}$ thirds	$\frac{?}{13}$ thirteenths	$\frac{?}{23}$ twenty-thirds
$\frac{?}{4}$ quarters	$\frac{?}{14}$ fourteenths	$\frac{?}{24}$ twenty-fourths
$\frac{?}{5}$ fifths	$\frac{?}{15}$ fifteenths	$\frac{?}{25}$ twenty-fifths
$\frac{?}{6}$ sixths	$\frac{?}{16}$ sixteenths	$\frac{?}{26}$ twenty-sixths
$\frac{?}{7}$ sevenths	$\frac{?}{17}$ seventeenths	$\frac{?}{27}$ twenty-sevenths
$\frac{?}{8}$ eighths	$\frac{?}{18}$ eighteenths	$\frac{?}{50}$ fiftieths
$\frac{?}{9}$ ninths	$\frac{?}{19}$ nineteenths	$\frac{?}{100}$ hundredths
$\frac{?}{10}$ tenths	$\frac{?}{20}$ twentieths	$\frac{?}{1000}$ thousandths
$\frac{?}{11}$ elevenths	$\frac{?}{21}$ twenty-oneths	$\frac{?}{1000000}$ millionths

Exercise 7b Write the following fractions in words using the list above for spelling:

1. $\frac{1}{2}$	7. $\frac{6}{7}$	13. $\frac{7}{8}$	19. $\frac{8}{11}$	25. $\frac{11}{19}$
2. $\frac{3}{4}$	8. $\frac{3}{16}$	14. $\frac{2}{9}$	20. $\frac{5}{12}$	26. $\frac{16}{23}$
3. $\frac{4}{5}$	9. $\frac{5}{18}$	15. $\frac{5}{9}$	21. $\frac{11}{12}$	27. $\frac{17}{20}$
4. $\frac{3}{8}$	10. $\frac{1}{20}$	16. $\frac{3}{10}$	22. $\frac{12}{13}$	28. $\frac{21}{40}$
5. $\frac{2}{3}$	11. $\frac{2}{7}$	17. $\frac{9}{10}$	23. $\frac{9}{14}$	29. $\frac{27}{50}$
6. $\frac{3}{5}$	12. $\frac{1}{8}$	18. $\frac{4}{11}$	24. $\frac{13}{15}$	30. $\frac{7}{100}$

Exercise 7c How many of each fraction are there in one whole:

1. halves	11. $\frac{1}{2}$	21. $\frac{1}{25}$
2. thirds	12. $\frac{1}{4}$	22. $\frac{1}{11}$
3. quarters	13. $\frac{1}{9}$	23. $\frac{1}{29}$
4. fifths	14. $\frac{1}{8}$	24. $\frac{1}{32}$
5. sixths	15. $\frac{1}{3}$	25. $\frac{1}{36}$
6. eighths	16. $\frac{1}{5}$	26. $\frac{1}{50}$
7. tenths	17. $\frac{1}{7}$	27. $\frac{1}{100}$
8. twelfths	18. $\frac{1}{16}$	28. $\frac{1}{200}$
9. fifteenths	19. $\frac{1}{18}$	29. $\frac{1}{250}$
10. twenty-fourths	20. $\frac{1}{20}$	30. $\frac{1}{1000}$

Numerator

The number on top in a fraction is called the **Numerator**. It tells us the number of parts we are using named by the denominator.

For example, $\frac{3}{4}$ is three lots of one quarter.

$\frac{1}{4}$ **is shaded** $\frac{3}{4}$ **is shaded**

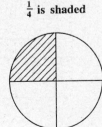 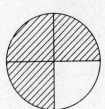

Exercise 7d State what fraction of the following shapes is shaded:

1.
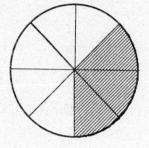

5.
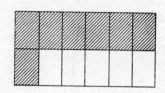

2.
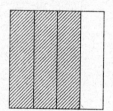

6.
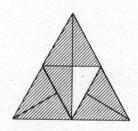

3.
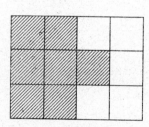

7.
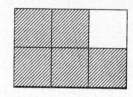

4.
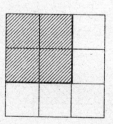

8.
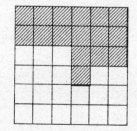

Finding a fraction of a quantity

To find a fraction of a quantity we divide the quantity by the denominator and multiply by the numerator. The sutra used here is *Proportionately*.

Find $\frac{1}{3}$ of 18 pencils.	The denominator is 3 and so we divide 18 by 3.
$18 \div 3 = 6$	3 into 18 goes 6. The numerator is 1 and $6 \times 1 = 6$, and so $\frac{1}{3}$ of 18 pencils is
<u>6 pencils</u>	6 pencils.
Find $\frac{3}{4}$ of 28 centimetres.	The denominator is 4 and so we divide 28 by 4. 4 into 28 goes 7.
$28 \div 4 = 7$	The numerator is 3 and $7 \times 3 = 21$, and so $\frac{3}{4}$ of 28 cm is 21 cm.
$7 \times 3 = 21$	
<u>21 centimetres</u>	

Exercise 7e Write answers only.

1. One half of 12
2. One half of 16
3. One half of 100
4. One third of 6
5. One third of 24
6. One quarter of 16
7. One quarter of 40
8. One tenth of 30
9. One fifth of 25
10. One sixth of 42

11. $\frac{1}{2}$ of 24
12. $\frac{1}{2}$ of 48
13. $\frac{1}{3}$ of 12
14. $\frac{1}{3}$ of 60
15. $\frac{1}{3}$ of 33
16. $\frac{1}{4}$ of 24
17. $\frac{1}{4}$ of 100
18. $\frac{1}{4}$ of 4
19. $\frac{1}{5}$ of 10
20. $\frac{1}{5}$ of 45

21. $\frac{1}{2}$ of 14 apples
22. $\frac{1}{2}$ of 20 cm
23. $\frac{1}{3}$ of £6.00
24. $\frac{1}{3}$ of 12 pencils
25. $\frac{1}{4}$ of 28 boys
26. $\frac{3}{4}$ of 400 m
27. $\frac{3}{8}$ of 16 cakes
28. $\frac{2}{9}$ of £72.00
29. $\frac{3}{10}$ of 20 plates
30. $\frac{7}{10}$ of £1.00

Exercise 7f Problems

1. Peter had 30 marbles and gave away half of them to Nancy. How many marbles did he have left?

2. Peter gave one third of the marbles he had left to Jonathan. How many marbles did he have left now?

3. Hannah read one half of her reading book in a day. If the book has 64 pages, how many pages did she read?

4. Mr Walker cycles 12 miles to work. If he stops for a rest after one quarter of this journey, how many miles has he left to cycle?

5. One fifth of the days in April were rainy. On how many days did it rain in April?

6. One cake is shared between three boys. What fraction of the whole cake does each boy receive?

7. If two cakes are shared between three boys, what fraction of a cake would each boy receive?

8. Mr Peasbody weighs 80 kilograms. What is one quarter of this weight?

9. Mrs Peasbody weighs three-quarters of what her husband weighs. How heavy is Mrs Peasbody?

10. A pearl necklace, with 30 pearls, breaks and one third of them scatter onto the floor. How many fell onto the floor?

11. If one fifth of the pearls on the floor could not be found, how many were found?

12. A recipe for bread requires one-thirtieth of the quantity of flour to be the quantity of yeast. If there is to be 60 ounces of flour, how much yeast is needed?

13. A batsman for a cricket team scores two-fifths of his teams total number of runs. If the team scored 150 runs, how many did the batsman score?

14. Geoffrey has £12. He spends one third of it on a present for his mother and a quarter of the remainder on a book. How much does he have left?

15. A pack of 52 playing cards is dealt out amongst four players. How many cards does each receive and what fraction of the whole pack does each player have?

Adding Fractions

Fractions can be added together when the denominators are the same.

$$\frac{3}{5} + \frac{1}{5} = \frac{4}{5}$$

In this example, the denominators are the same. To add these two fractions just add the two numerators together, 3 + 1 = 4.

Exercise 7g Add:

1. $\frac{1}{4} + \frac{1}{4}$

2. $\frac{1}{3} + \frac{1}{3}$

3. $\frac{1}{9} + \frac{7}{9}$

4. $\frac{1}{4} + \frac{2}{4}$

5. $\frac{1}{5} + \frac{2}{5}$

6. $\frac{1}{5} + \frac{1}{5}$

7. $\frac{1}{7} + \frac{2}{7}$

8. $\frac{1}{12} + \frac{6}{12}$

9. $\frac{1}{8} + \frac{3}{8}$

10. $\frac{2}{9} + \frac{5}{9}$

11. $\frac{1}{7} + \frac{3}{7}$

12. $\frac{2}{7} + \frac{4}{7}$

13. $\frac{3}{10} + \frac{1}{10}$

14. $\frac{1}{6} + \frac{1}{6}$

15. $\frac{3}{5} + \frac{1}{5}$

16. $\frac{1}{9} + \frac{1}{9}$

17. $\frac{2}{9} + \frac{4}{9}$

18. $\frac{1}{5} + \frac{3}{5}$

19. $\frac{1}{10} + \frac{6}{10}$

20. $\frac{1}{8} + \frac{1}{8}$

Equivalent Fractions

Two fractions are equivalent when their numerators and denominators are different but the value or size of the fractions is the same. For example, two quarters is the same size as one half. The diagram below shows this.

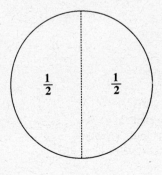
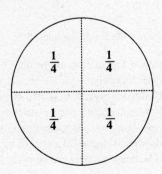

The fraction strips below show halves, quarters, eighths and sixteenths.

We can see that $\frac{1}{2} = \frac{2}{4}$, $\frac{1}{4} = \frac{2}{8}$, and so on. These are equivalent fractions.

1							

$\frac{1}{2}$				$\frac{1}{2}$			

$\frac{1}{4}$		$\frac{1}{4}$		$\frac{1}{4}$		$\frac{1}{4}$	

$\frac{1}{8}$	$\frac{1}{8}$	$\frac{1}{8}$	$\frac{1}{8}$	$\frac{1}{8}$	$\frac{1}{8}$	$\frac{1}{8}$	$\frac{1}{8}$

$\frac{1}{16}$	$\frac{1}{16}$	$\frac{1}{16}$	$\frac{1}{16}$	$\frac{1}{16}$	$\frac{1}{16}$	$\frac{1}{16}$	$\frac{1}{16}$	$\frac{1}{16}$	$\frac{1}{16}$	$\frac{1}{16}$	$\frac{1}{16}$	$\frac{1}{16}$	$\frac{1}{16}$	$\frac{1}{16}$	$\frac{1}{16}$

Exercise 7h Use the diagram above to write down the equivalent fraction.

1. $\frac{1}{2} = \frac{?}{4}$

2. $\frac{2}{2} = \frac{?}{4}$

3. $\frac{2}{8} = \frac{?}{4}$

4. $\frac{2}{4} = \frac{?}{8}$

5. $\frac{1}{8} = \frac{?}{16}$

6. $\frac{3}{4} = \frac{?}{8}$

7. $\frac{4}{8} = \frac{?}{4}$

8. $\frac{4}{16} = \frac{?}{8}$

9. $\frac{3}{4} = \frac{?}{8}$

10. $\frac{6}{16} = \frac{?}{8}$

11. $\frac{1}{4} = \frac{?}{16}$

12. $\frac{8}{16} = \frac{?}{8}$

13. $\frac{3}{4} = \frac{?}{16}$

14. $\frac{5}{8} = \frac{?}{16}$

15. $\frac{3}{8} = \frac{6}{?}$

16. $\frac{14}{16} = \frac{?}{8}$

17. $\frac{2}{4} = \frac{?}{16}$

18. $\frac{12}{16} = \frac{?}{8}$

19. $\frac{1}{4} = \frac{4}{?}$

20. $\frac{7}{8} = \frac{14}{?}$

Now answer the following questions:

21. How many quarters can fit into one half?
22. How many eigths can fit into one quarter?
23. How many eigths can fit into one half?
24. How many eigths can fit into three quarters?
25. How many sixteenths can fit into three eigths?
26. How many eigths can be made up from four sixteenths?
27. How many quarters can be made up from twelve sixteenths?

The next diagram shows fraction strips where one is divided into thirds, then sixths and then twelfths.

Exercise 7i Use the diagram above to write down the equivalent fraction.

1. $\dfrac{1}{3} = \dfrac{?}{6}$

6. $\dfrac{4}{6} = \dfrac{?}{12}$

11. $\dfrac{2}{3} = \dfrac{?}{12}$

16. $1 = \dfrac{?}{3}$

2. $\dfrac{3}{3} = \dfrac{?}{6}$

7. $\dfrac{1}{3} = \dfrac{?}{12}$

12. $\dfrac{3}{3} = \dfrac{?}{12}$

17. $\dfrac{10}{12} = \dfrac{5}{?}$

3. $\dfrac{2}{3} = \dfrac{?}{6}$

8. $\dfrac{4}{12} = \dfrac{?}{6}$

13. $\dfrac{5}{6} = \dfrac{?}{12}$

18. $\dfrac{2}{6} = \dfrac{4}{?}$

4. $\dfrac{1}{6} = \dfrac{?}{12}$

9. $\dfrac{3}{6} = \dfrac{?}{12}$

14. $\dfrac{1}{3} = \dfrac{2}{?}$

19. $1 = \dfrac{12}{?}$

5. $\dfrac{2}{6} = \dfrac{?}{12}$

10. $\dfrac{6}{12} = \dfrac{?}{6}$

15. $\dfrac{6}{6} = \dfrac{?}{12}$

20. $\dfrac{8}{12} = \dfrac{2}{?}$

21. How many thirds can fit into one whole?
22. How many sixths can fit into one third?
23. How many sixths can fit into two thirds?
24. How many twelfths can fit into one third?
25. How many twelfths can fit into two thirds?
26. How many thirds can be made up from four twelfths?
27. How many sixths can be made up from six twelfths?
28. How many sixths can be made up from ten twelfths?
29. How many thirds can be made up from eight twelfths?
30. How many thirds can be made up from two twelfths added to six sixths?

Fractions to Infinity

Take a piece of A4 size paper and a pair of scissors. Fold the piece of paper exactly in half, corner to corner, edge to edge, and crease. Open the paper, press flat and cut along the fold. There are now two halves. Write $\frac{1}{2}$ on one piece and set it aside. Now carefully fold one piece in half, open up and cut along the fold. Each piece is one quarter of the whole. Write the fraction $\frac{1}{4}$ on one piece and set it aside.

Continue in this way, folding one piece in half and setting the other aside, until you cannot go any further. What fraction of the the first piece of paper have you reached down to?

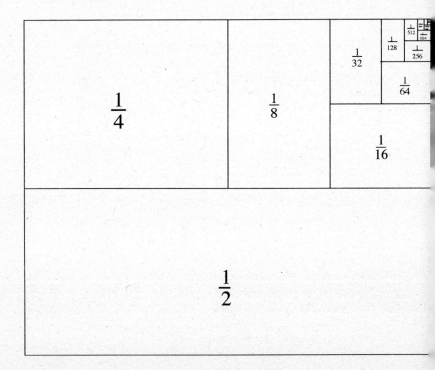

The principle here is that whenever there is multiplication there is division, and vice versa; whenever there is addition there is subtraction, and vice versa. Can you see why it is that whenever there is division there must be multiplication?

Exercise 7j Now answer the following questions:

1. How many halves are there in a one whole?
2. How many quarters are there in one whole?
3. How many quarters are there in one half?
4. How many eigths are there in one whole?
5. How many eigths are there in one quarter?
6. How many eigths are there in one half?
7. How many sixteenths are there in one half?
8. How many sixteenths are there in one eigth?
9. How many sixteenths are there in one quarter?
10. What is one half divided by two?
11. What is one quarter divided by two?
12. What is one sixteenth divided by two?
13. What is one half divided by four?
14. What is one quarter divided by four?
15. What is the bottom number in a fraction called?
16. What is the top number in a fraction called?
17. What happens with the denominator each time a fraction is cut in half?
18. If it were possible, and we carried on dividing forever what would the denominator be?

In the Katha Upanishad we hear,

"The Self is lesser than the least, greater than the greatest. He lives in all hearts. When the senses are at rest, free from desire, man finds Him and mounts beyond sorrow."

[Trans. Yeats]

Chapter Eight - Decimal Fractions

Decimal fractions are based on tenths, hundredths, thousands, and so on, all of which are unity, or one, with different numbers of noughts. Instead of using a numerator and denominator decimal fractions use place value or number columns.

The first decimal fraction is one tenth and is written as 0.1. The 0 means no units and the 1 stands for one tenth. The dot in between the 0 and the 1 is called the decimal point. This decimal point distinguishes whole, on the left, from parts, on the right.

One tenth $= \frac{1}{10} = 0.1$

Two tenths $= \frac{2}{10} = 0.2$

Three tenths $= \frac{3}{10} = 0.3$

Four tenths $= \frac{4}{10} = 0.4$

Five tenths $= \frac{5}{10} = 0.5$

Six tenths $= \frac{6}{10} = 0.6$

Seven tenths $= \frac{7}{10} = 0.7$

Eight tenths $= \frac{8}{10} = 0.8$

Nine tenths $= \frac{9}{10} = 0.9$

Ten tenths $= \frac{10}{10} = 1.0 = 1$

The decimal point is the point which separates wholes, on the left, from parts, on the right. There is a story which illustrates this separating things off.

There was an impatient man in India who wanted to realise God. So he went to a holy man to ask for help. The holy man said that all he needed to do was to remember that God is in everything and means no harm and then he would realise God. So the man happily went on his way busily remembering that God is in everything.

On his way home he was walking down a narrow country lane with high hedges on either side. He suddenly saw an elephant coming in the opposite direction. Sitting on top of the elephant was an elephant driver who, seeing the man cried out, "Get out of the way!"

Seeing that there was no room to get past the man said to himself, "God is in me, God is in the elephant. Can God harm God? No!". And he carried on walking towards the elephant. The elephant driver again called for him to get out of the way and again the man said to himself, "God is in me, God is in the elephant. Can God harm God? No!", and carried on going. As soon as the elephant reached the man it picked him up in his trunk and threw him over the hedge.

Hurt and sorrowful the man returned to the holy teacher and told him of his experience. The holy man said, "You were quite right to remember that God is in you and God is in the elephant, but God is also in the elephant driver and he told you to get out of the way!".

This story illustrates how easy it is to forget the whole by separating things off into parts.

Naming, reading and writing decimal numbers

The first practice with decimals is that of counting. Practice counting in decimals. Start with 0.1 and count up to 2.5 in tenths; nought point one, nought point two, etc. Also practice counting in hundredths starting at 0.01.

This table shows some decimal numbers. The first column after the decimal point is for tenths, the second column is for hundredths, and so on.

	Number	Hundreds 100	Tens 10	Units 1		Tenths $\frac{1}{10}$	Hundredths $\frac{1}{100}$	Thousandths $\frac{1}{1000}$
A	4.7			4	.	7		
B	5.16			5	.	1	6	
C	23.67		2	3	.	6	7	
D	41.741		4	1	.	7	4	1
E	347.619	3	4	7	.	6	1	9
F	420.071	4	2	0	.	0	7	1
G	100.001	1	0	0	.	0	0	1

How the numbers in the table are spoken is shown below:-

A. Four point seven,
B. Five point one six (not five point sixteen),
C. Twenty-three point six seven (not twenty-three point sixty seven),
D. Forty-one point seven four one,
E. Three hundred and forty-seven point six one nine,
F. Four hundred and twenty point nought seven one,
G. One hundred point nought nought one.

Exercise 8a

How many tenths are there in each of the following:

1. 0.2	4. 1.1	7. 0.1	10. 2.3	13. 2.5
2. 0.5	5. 1.6	8. 1.2	11. 0.9	14. 3.4
3. 0.8	6. 1.9	9. 0.7	12. 1.9	15. 4.2

How many hundredths are there in each of the following:

16. 0.02	19. 0.12	22. 0.23	25. 2.31	28. 3.05
17. 0.05	20. 0.35	23. 0.40	26. 0.99	29. 2.19
18. 0.08	21. 0.01	24. 0.7	27. 7.31	30. 4.2

Exercise 8b Reading and writing decimal numbers

Write the following decimals in words:

1. 2.3	4. 0.8	7. 3.24	10. 2.05	13. 9.24
2. 4.4	5. 0.4	8. 5.18	11. 34.5	14. 567.23
3. 1.7	6. 0.2	9. 9.63	12. 76.1	15. 1.407

Write the following as decimal numbers:

16. Two point three
17. Three point seven
18. Nought point two
19. Five point six seven
20. One point nought five

21. Sixty-two point three
22. Fifty point three
23. Ninety-five point one
24. Six hundred and four point two
25. Nought point four nought three

Addition of decimals

When adding decimal numbers vertically the decimal points must be in line with each other. Other than the decimal point the addition of decimal numbers is the same as the addition of whole numbers.

Example　4.5　　The decimal points are kept in line.
　　　　　+ 2.3
　　　　　 6.8　　The decimal point in the answer is also in line.

Exercise 8c Addition without carrying; write answers only:

1.	2.1 +1.1	11.	0.2 +0.5	21.	5.1 +3.0	31.	3.3 +2.6
2.	4.4 +4.1	12.	1.2 +2.4	22.	3.1 +1.4	32.	1.3 +2.1
3.	1.1 +3.0	13.	4.1 +5.2	23.	4.1 +2.4	33.	3.2 +2.1
4.	3.4 +1.4	14.	7.3 +2.4	24.	5.2 +3.7	34.	3.5 +3.1
5.	2.0 +2.2	15.	6.5 +2.4	25.	3.2 +2.3	35.	4.6 +5.1
6.	2.4 +2.3	16.	0.1 +3.8	26.	1.1 +4.7	36.	3.4 +1.5
7.	5.9 +4.0	17.	4.0 +3.3	27.	4.1 +3.8	37.	2.1 +3.5
8.	4.0 +1.8	18.	1.5 +0.4	28.	3.1 +5.1	38.	4.2 +2.4
9.	3.1 +3.1	19.	3.8 +6.1	29.	3.7 +3.2	39.	4.1 +3.7
10.	3.7 +3.1	20.	4.3 +2.5	30.	4.3 +3.3	40.	2.5 +5.4

When the digits in a particular column add up to ten or more then carry to the left as with the addition of ordinary numbers. The example below shows this. Remember to place the decimal points one below the other.

Example	7.8	8 + 3 = 11, put down 1 and carry 1.
	+ 8.3	7 + 8 = 15, 15 + 1 = 16, put down 6
	16.1	and carry 1.
	11	

Exercise 8d Addition with carrying:

1.	1.5 +1.5	11.	2.9 +1.9	21.	2.7 +2.5	31.	6.3 +7.7
2.	3.3 +2.8	12.	4.9 +4.7	22.	3.9 +3.7	32.	7.8 +5.4
3.	4.9 +3.8	13.	5.7 +2.8	23.	2.8 +2.3	33.	6.9 +8.6
4.	4.7 +3.8	14.	4.3 +3.8	24.	2.9 +3.7	34.	8.5 +3.5
5.	2.7 +2.3	15.	3.5 +3.9	25.	5.6 +7.1	35.	4.6 +5.4
6.	3.9 +3.9	16.	3.3 +3.9	26.	9.0 +4.7	36.	7.7 +2.3
7.	3.5 +2.8	17.	2.8 +3.2	27.	8.6 +5.2	37.	2.1 +7.9
8.	3.9 +2.9	18.	4.9 +4.5	28.	2.1 +9.1	38.	4.6 +8.8
9.	4.1 +4.9	19.	8.6 +0.7	29.	8.7 +7.2	39.	9.8 +9.8
10.	2.9 +3.3	20.	2.8 +2.7	30.	9.3 +9.3	40.	2.5 +8.7

Column addition with decimals

Find the sum of 3.4, 5.8, 6.7 and 8.4

3.4	The sum is set out with the decimal
5.8	points in a vertical line.
6.7	4 + 8 + 7 + 4 = 23, put down 3 and
+ 8.4	carry 2.
24.3	3 + 5 + 6 + 8 + 2 = 24
22	

Exercise 8e Set these out vertically with the decimal points in line:

1. 2.9 + 2.1 + 1.9 + 1.1

2. 1.9 + 2.8 + 1.7 + 1.4

3. 2.9 + 1.1 + 1.3 + 2.8

4. 1.9 + 3.5 + 0.9 + 2.5

5. 0.7 + 1.6 + 3.4 + 4.3

6. 1.2 + 2.3 + 3.5 + 0.9

7. 2.5 + 1.5 + 2.5 + 1.5

8. 2.9 + 1.9 + 1.5 + 1.5

9. 1.7 + 1.5 + 3.1 + 2.9

10. 1.1 + 2.8 + 2.7 + 2.3

11. 2.7 + 0.3 + 1.6 + 0.4

12. 0.8 + 0.3 + 0.7 + 0.5

13. 0.6 + 2.7 + 0.7 + 2.6

14. 2.4 + 2.4 + 2.4 + 2.4

15. 4.7 + 2.1 + 7.9 + 4.5 + 3.3

16. 3.45 + 7.09 + 4.58

17. 61.3 + 21.5 + 30.6

18. 81.2 + 58.4 + 40.5

19. 29.1 + 4.3 + 27.5

20. 79.6 + 5.8 + 34.8

21. 0.76 + 0.06 + 0.31

22. 0.882 + 0.372 + 0.212

23. 1.980 + 2.343 + 3.4 + 6.87

24. 5.43 + 3.81 + 0.33

25. 456.2 + 203.6 + 554.1

26. 546.2 + 1.121 + 653.2

27. 87.23 + 12.34 + 78.07

28. 76.33 + 66.21 + 82.82

29. 2.45 + 34.76 + 1.234

30. 2.987 + 3.2 + 54.98

Subtraction of decimals

Exercise 8f Subtraction without complements; write answers only:

1.	8.6 −1.5	11.	2.9 −1.9	21.	2.7 −2.5	31.	8.5 −7.4
2.	4.9 −2.8	12.	4.9 −4.7	22.	3.9 −3.7	32.	7.8 −5.4
3.	4.9 −3.8	13.	5.8 −2.2	23.	2.8 −2.3	33.	8.9 −6.6
4.	4.8 −3.8	14.	9.6 −3.3	24.	8.9 −3.7	34.	8.5 −3.5
5.	2.7 −2.3	15.	7.5 −3.1	25.	5.6 −4.1	35.	5.6 −4.4
6.	3.9 −1.4	16.	8.3 −5.3	26.	9.0 −4.0	36.	7.7 −2.3
7.	3.5 −2.1	17.	7.8 −3.2	27.	8.6 −5.2	37.	7.9 −2.1
8.	3.9 −2.6	18.	4.9 −4.5	28.	9.1 −8.1	38.	8.8 −4.6
9.	4.1 −2.0	19.	8.7 −0.6	29.	8.7 −7.2	39.	9.8 −1.1
10.	2.9 −1.3	20.	6.8 −2.7	30.	9.3 −9.3	40.	2.5 −0.4

Exercise 8g Find out whether to add or take away and then set out the sum:

1. What is 3.5 added to 6.9?

2. Which is larger, 2.4 or 5.1?

3. Subtract 2.4 from 9.7

4. Find the total of 5.6, and 7.1

5. Which is larger, 3.42 or 3.6?

6. Take 4.1 away from 8.6

7. What is the sum of 5.4 and 1.8?

8. Subtract 4.5 from 12.7

9. By how much is 2.3 larger than 1.2?

10. Add together 5.5, 4.6 and 7.2

11. Take 8.7 away from 12.9

12. Find the difference between 34.6 and 21.3

Nikhilam subtraction is also used for decimals.

Example	7.1	Difference between 1 and 9 is 8, complement, 2.
	− 3.9	7 − 3 = 4, drop 1 gives 3.
	3.2	The answer is 3.2

Exercise 8h Nikhilam subtraction:

1.	2.1 −1.3	11.	2.0 −0.3	21.	5.1 −3.9	31.	2.1 −1.4
2.	3.2 −1.3	12.	9.3 −5.9	22.	2.0 −1.4	32.	1.1 −0.4
3.	2.0 −0.5	13.	2.1 −1.5	23.	5.4 −2.8	33.	2.1 −0.6
4.	2.0 −1.6	14.	6.3 −1.9	24.	8.4 −3.8	34.	2.1 −1.7
5.	3.0 −0.7	15.	3.2 −1.6	25.	4.3 −2.4	35.	8.7 −3.8
6.	9.5 −4.7	16.	5.4 −2.9	26.	9.1 −6.6	36.	7.6 −2.8
7.	6.5 −1.6	17.	3.2 −1.5	27.	9.4 −6.5	37.	3.1 −1.4
8.	6.3 −1.8	18.	5.4 −2.7	28.	7.1 −4.2	38.	8.2 −2.8
9.	7.3 −4.8	19.	4.1 −2.9	29.	4.3 −2.8	39.	8.4 −3.6
10.	8.0 −1.3	20.	6.0 −0.1	30.	7.0 −0.3	40.	5.0 −0.4

Vedic Mathematics for Schools 1

Using nought to fill the space

Nought, or zero, is very full although it looks quite empty. In decimal fractions we can use nought to fill spaces to make calculations easier.

With a number like 0.5 the 5 stands for five tenths. Since there are no hundredths this is the same as 0.50. 0.50 means five tenths and no hundredths. Furthermore, since there are no thousandths 0.50 is the same as 0.500. 0.500 means five tenths, no hundredths and no thousandths.

In fact we could write 0.5 as 0.50000000000000000000000000000000000000000 and it would still stand for five tenths and nothing else.

With decimal fractions it is often useful to fill empty spaces with noughts just to remind us that there is nothing there.

Example: Subtract 7.87 from 52.1
Notice that noughts are placed where there are no numbers

$$\begin{array}{r} 52.10 \\ -\ 07.87 \\ \hline 44.23 \end{array}$$

Exercise 8i Nikhilam subtraction:

1. $\begin{array}{r}17.6\\-\ 4.85\end{array}$	6. $\begin{array}{r}19.41\\-\ 6.82\end{array}$	11. $\begin{array}{r}31.8\\-12.93\end{array}$	16. $\begin{array}{r}2.417\\-1.209\end{array}$
2. $\begin{array}{r}15.72\\-\ 9.29\end{array}$	7. $\begin{array}{r}2.47\\-1.375\end{array}$	12. $\begin{array}{r}3.5\\-1.824\end{array}$	17. $\begin{array}{r}5.1\\-4.982\end{array}$
3. $\begin{array}{r}13.8\\-\ 2.96\end{array}$	8. $\begin{array}{r}2.35\\-0.671\end{array}$	13. $\begin{array}{r}0.463\\-0.295\end{array}$	18. $\begin{array}{r}57.1\\-28.07\end{array}$
4. $\begin{array}{r}2.746\\-0.89\end{array}$	9. $\begin{array}{r}32.71\\-19.07\end{array}$	14. $\begin{array}{r}0.42\\-0.228\end{array}$	19. $\begin{array}{r}1.53\\-0.444\end{array}$
5. $\begin{array}{r}2.527\\-1.643\end{array}$	10. $\begin{array}{r}3.312\\-1.746\end{array}$	15. $\begin{array}{r}3.442\\-1.076\end{array}$	20. $\begin{array}{r}5.241\\-4.953\end{array}$

21. From 23.763 subtract 16.105

22. From 37.312 subtract 25.534

23. From 41.135 subtract 37.213

24. Subtract 74.317 from 83.125

25. Subtract 83.618 from 91.595

26. Subtract 92.05 from 101.79

Multiplication of decimals

When one number is a decimal but the other is a whole number the decimal point in the answer is placed in line with the decimal point above.

```
Example        7.1      4 × 1 = 4
             ×    4      4 × 7 = 28
              28.4      The answer is 28.4
```

Exercise 8j Multiply:

1. 2.1 × 3	11. 2.4 × 3	21. 5.1 × 4	31. 2.1 × 9
2. 3.2 × 3	12. 9.3 × 7	22. 2.8 × 4	32. 8.1 × 4
3. 2.1 × 5	13. 2.1 × 5	23. 5.2 × 8	33. 2.6 × 6
4. 3.1 × 6	14. 6.8 × 6	24. 8.4 × 3	34. 2.2 × 7
5. 3.2 × 7	15. 3.2 × 7	25. 4.3 × 7	35. 8.7 × 8
6. 9.5 × 2	16. 5.4 × 9	26. 9.1 × 6	36. 7.6 × 8
7. 6.2 × 6	17. 3.2 × 5	27. 9.4 × 5	37. 3.8 × 4
8. 6.3 × 4	18. 5.5 × 7	28. 7.1 × 6	38. 8.2 × 8
9. 7.3 × 5	19. 4.1 × 8	29. 4.3 × 8	39. 8.4 × 6
10. 8.0 × 3	20. 6.0 × 1	30. 7.2 × 3	40. 5.6 × 4

Vedic Mathematics for Schools 1

Exercise 8k Multiply:

1. 0.55 × 2	**11.** 1.23 × 3	**21.** 21.34 × 3	**31.** 0.86 × 4
2. 0.42 × 3	**12.** 1.54 × 5	**22.** 34.56 × 4	**32.** 2.35 × 6
3. 0.28 × 4	**13.** 1.68 × 6	**23.** 51.03 × 6	**33.** 56.1 × 7
4. 0.34 × 5	**14.** 1.86 × 7	**24.** 23.4 × 4	**34.** 73.23 × 3
5. 0.47 × 3	**15.** 3.68 × 4	**25.** 56.12 × 8	**35.** 3.67 × 7
6. 0.61 × 4	**16.** 4.96 × 6	**26.** 17.8 × 9	**36.** 0.76 × 4
7. 0.73 × 5	**17.** 6.65 × 8	**27.** 35.71 × 7	**37.** 1.34 × 4
8. 0.66 × 6	**18.** 7.86 × 9	**28.** 21.06 × 6	**38.** 9.55 × 7
9. 0.81 × 7	**19.** 2.56 × 6	**29.** 66.7 × 4	**39.** 25.55 × 5
10. 0.76 × 4	**20.** 1.78 × 5	**30.** 38.91 × 7	**40.** 917.3 × 6

Multiplying and dividing by multiples of ten

To multiply a decimal number by ten we move the decimal point one place to the right. To multiply a number by one hundred we move the decimal point two places to the right. Noughts may have to be added to fill the empty places.

5 × 10 = 50	5 × 100 = 500
3.45 × 10 = 34.5	3.45 × 100 = 345
0.4 × 10 = 4.0	0.4 × 100 = 40
0.007 × 10 = 0.7	0.007 × 100 = 0.7

Exercise 8l

Multiply these numbers by 10

1. 2	**6.** 1.23	**11.** 0.7	**16.** 1.02
2. 34	**7.** 12.5	**12.** 9.9	**17.** 23.9
3. 234	**8.** 3.4	**13.** 1.234	**18.** 2.005
4. 2.34	**9.** 4.5	**14.** 765.45	**19.** 0.145
5. 7.44	**10.** 0.5	**15.** 45.7	**20.** 0.004

Exercise 8m

Multiply these numbers by 100

1. 2	**6.** 11.234	**11.** 0.06	**16.** 12.5
2. 34	**7.** 12.577	**12.** 2.3	**17.** 56.3
3. 234	**8.** 3.487	**13.** 0.3	**18.** 4.264
4. 2.314	**9.** 4.51	**14.** 765.45	**19.** 0.145
5. 7.444	**10.** 0.554	**15.** 45.7	**20.** 0.004

To divide a decimal number by ten we move the decimal point one place to the left. To divide a number by one hundred we move the decimal point two places to the left. Noughts may have to be added to fill the empty places.

$$500 \div 10 = 50 \qquad\qquad 500 \div 100 = 5$$
$$345 \div 10 = 34.5 \qquad\qquad 345 \div 100 = 3.45$$
$$43.7 \div 10 = 4.37 \qquad\qquad 43.7 \div 100 = 0.437$$
$$7 \div 10 = 0.7 \qquad\qquad 0.7 \div 100 = 0.007$$

Exercise 8n

Divide these numbers by 10

1. 60	**6.** 58.7	**11.** 0.5	**16.** 0.05
2. 340	**7.** 87.4	**12.** 23.77	**17.** 0.4
3. 2340	**8.** 65.0	**13.** 1.26	**18.** 38.09
4. 400	**9.** 34.0	**14.** 485.41	**19.** 0.001
5. 12.3	**10.** 3	**15.** 40.3	**20.** 0.564

Exercise 8p

Divide these numbers by 100

1. 300	**6.** 465.7	**11.** 65.0	**16.** 19.5
2. 3400	**7.** 879.01	**12.** 57.1	**17.** 5.3
3. 234.3	**8.** 237.3	**13.** 28.6	**18.** 0.8
4. 546.3	**9.** 56.1	**14.** 765.45	**19.** 0.56
5. 5463.2	**10.** 76.87	**15.** 4.5	**20.** 0.09

Division of decimals

As long as the divisor is a whole number the decimal point in the answer is placed so as to be in line with the decimal point of the dividend. Except for the decimal point the dividing is done in the same way as for ordinary division.

Example $\quad 4\,\lfloor 83.24$ $\qquad$ 4 into 8 = 2
$\qquad\qquad\underline{\quad 3\quad}$ $\qquad\qquad$ 4 into 3 = 0 remainder 3
$\qquad\qquad\quad 20.81$ $\qquad\qquad$ 4 into 32 = 8
$\qquad\qquad\qquad\qquad\qquad$ 4 into 4 = 1

Exercise 8q Division

1. $3\lfloor 3.6$	**7.** $3\lfloor 3.9$	**13.** $8\lfloor 6.4$	**19.** $3\lfloor 9.513$	**25.** $6\lfloor 3.612$
2. $2\lfloor 4.8$	**8.** $6\lfloor 6.18$	**14.** $7\lfloor 3.5$	**20.** $4\lfloor 16.24$	**26.** $4\lfloor 0.468$
3. $4\lfloor 8.8$	**9.** $4\lfloor 4.28$	**15.** $4\lfloor 6.8$	**21.** $5\lfloor 2.785$	**27.** $3\lfloor 0.312$
4. $3\lfloor 6.9$	**10.** $7\lfloor 7.14$	**16.** $6\lfloor 7.2$	**22.** $2\lfloor 6.312$	**28.** $2\lfloor 0.572$
5. $2\lfloor 2.0$	**11.** $2\lfloor 6.46$	**17.** $3\lfloor 6.3$	**23.** $6\lfloor 12.78$	**29.** $4\lfloor 2.840$
6. $2\lfloor 8.6$	**12.** $3\lfloor 6.39$	**18.** $5\lfloor 2.5$	**24.** $2\lfloor 6.112$	**30.** $5\lfloor 375.5$

Working with money

Since there are one hundred pence in the pound decimals are used for calculations with money. When writing pounds and pence together there are always two figures after the decimal point. So 3 pounds 5 pence is written as £3.05.

Exercise 8r Write in figures:

1. One pound fifty
2. One pound forty
3. One pound fifteen

4. Three pounds twelve
5. One pound seven
6. One pound eight

7. Two pounds three
8. Five pounds sixty
9. Five pounds six

10. Two pounds ten   **12.** One pound one   **14.** Two pounds seven

11. Two pounds thirty   **13.** One pound five   **15.** Ten pounds ninety

When answering problems always read the question to find what type of sum is involved and then set out the sum in the correct way.

A girl goes into a shop and spends £2.15 on a pen, £1.85 on some ink and £2.99 on paper. How much does she spend altogether?

She spends £6.94

$$
\begin{array}{r}
£ \\
2.14 \\
1.85 \\
+\ 2.95 \\
\hline
6.94 \\
\hline
1\ 1
\end{array}
$$

Exercise 8s Problems

1. Mrs Potterabout spent £3.45 at the grocer, £5.73 in the hardware store and £3.48 at the post office. How much did she spend altogether?

2. Find the cost of 12 stamps at 25p each.

3. If I buy a pair of garden shears costing £13.85, how much change should I receive from a twenty pound note?

4. The entrance fee to a museum is £2.75 for adults and £1.25 for children. How much is the total fee for two adults and five children?

5. A five litre tin of paint costs £19.25. How much would three such tins cost?

6. Mr Spender has £345.95 in his bank account. If he withdraws £196.28, how much will he have left in the bank?

7. Jonathan saved all of his pocket money for six weeks and found that he had £19.50. How much does he receive each week?

8. A factory worker earns £25.75 per hour. How much does he earn in 8 hrs?

9. Find the cost of seven litres of milk at 38p per litre.

10. Find the total cost of 5 kg of apples at 85p per kilogram and 2 kg of oranges at 64p per kilogram.

Chapter Nine - The Meaning Of Numbers

In the Veda there are descriptions of the meaning of the nine numbers. In this cha we will look at some of these meanings.

To begin with, the creation is made of nine elements and each element stands number. The elements are shown on the circle of nine points. The basic num always remain one to nine and all extra numbers are only the product of these stages seen in different levels.

The number one is the Absolute, or God, from which everything comes. We are that this universe comes from the Absolute, is sustained by the Absolute and fir merges into the Absolute. Two stands for unmanifest nature and three for the man nature. At four there is the whole world of mind and the feeling of existence.

The physical world, which we can hear, touch, see, taste and smell, starts at num five. Number five stands for ether, or space, and has the quality of sound. Six i and has the quality of touch. Fire is at seven with the quality of light and water eight with the quality of taste and bonding. Finally, at nine is earth. It has smell crystalline form.

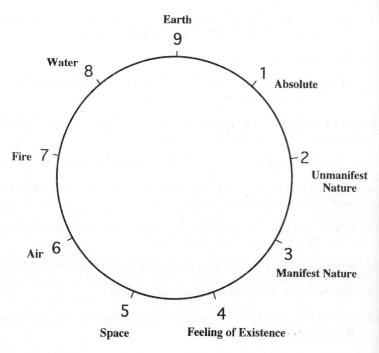

The Number One

> *"The ultimate or the Absolute (Brahman) is one and with the start of creation it unfolds itself in nine states and there it ends.*
>
> *"This universe is created by the Absolute, the creation of manifested forms is sustained by it, and in the end the whole creation will once again merge into it. That is the Brahman and that is what one needs to know."*
>
> [Sri Sankaracarya]

Just as the Absolute is inside everything so the number one is a factor of every number and every number is a factor of itself.

What is a factor? Before understanding what the word 'factor' means it is necessary to know what a product is.

Product

When numbers are multiplied together the answer is called the **product**. For example, $2 \times 7 = 14$; 14 is the product of 2 and 7.

Exercise 9a Write down the products of the following:-

1. 2×3	11. 8×7	21. 16×2
2. 5×4	12. 4×3	22. 25×4
3. 3×8	13. 7×3	23. 100×8
4. 6×7	14. 6×8	24. 4×15
5. 9×0	15. 12×8	25. 12×1
6. 7×7	16. 11×9	26. 7×1
7. 4×9	17. 6×0	27. 1×19
8. 12×2	18. 6×10	28. 257×1
9. 3×3	19. 13×2	29. 1×1
10. 5×11	20. 2×50	30. 1×38

You will notice that in the last six questions of this exercise the product of any number with one is always that number. In other words, multiplying by 1 brings about no change. The same is said in the Upanishads

> *"The Absolute is not the cause of any effect."*
>
> [Brihadaranyaka Upanishad II:V:18]

73

Factors

Numbers which are multiplied together to give a product are called **factors** of that product.

For example, 2 and 7 are factors of 14 because $14 = 2 \times 7$.

Exercise 9b Write each number as the product of two factors
Example: $15 = 5 \times 3$

1. 4	**7.** 10	**13.** 25	**19.** 64	**25.** 3
2. 6	**8.** 24	**14.** 40	**20.** 28	**26.** 5
3. 9	**9.** 16	**15.** 55	**21.** 50	**27.** 7
4. 18	**10.** 12	**16.** 72	**22.** 32	**28.** 11
5. 22	**11.** 36	**17.** 45	**23.** 35	**29.** 13
6. 8	**12.** 30	**18.** 56	**24.** 60	**30.** 19

In the last six questions of this exercise you will see that the only way to write each number as the product of two factors is to use 1 as one of the factors and the number itself as the other factor. In fact, we can do this for all numbers and we arrive at the one times table.

$$1 = 1 \times 1$$
$$2 = 1 \times 2$$
$$3 = 1 \times 3$$
$$4 = 1 \times 4, \text{ and so on for all numbers.}$$

The number one is a factor of every number in the same way that God is inside everything. A number may also be seen as a factor of itself. All numbers therefore have one and themselves as factors.

Some numbers have more than one pair of factors.

Example	List the factors of 24	$24 = 1 \times 24$
		$= 2 \times 12$
		$= 3 \times 8$
		$= 4 \times 6$

In this list we do not need to give 6×4, 8×3, etc., because $6 \times 4 = 4 \times 6$ and this has already been given.

Exercise 9c List the factors of the following:
(The number in brackets tells you how many <u>pairs</u> of factors.)

1.	6	(2)	**6.**	14	(2)	**11.**	21	(2)	**16.**	26	(2)
2.	8	(2)	**7.**	12	(3)	**12.**	33	(2)	**17.**	30	(4)
3.	9	(2)	**8.**	7	(1)	**13.**	11	(1)	**18.**	35	(2)
4.	10	(2)	**9.**	20	(3)	**14.**	5	(1)	**19.**	36	(5)
5.	15	(2)	**10.**	18	(3)	**15.**	16	(3)	**20.**	100	(5)

Divisibility

The number one is not a product and cannot be divided. It is indivisible. A number which is a product is divisible by any one of its factors. For example, 10 is the product of 2 and 5 and so 2 and 5 are factors of 10. 10 can be divided by 2 or 5 without any remainder.

$$10 \div 2 = 5$$
$$10 \div 5 = 2$$

As with multiplying by 1, when dividing a number by 1, there is no change. For example, $28 \div 1 = 28$. So, although we pretend that it does, the number one cannot really do any dividing at all.

"The Absolute is not the cause of any effect."

[Brihadaranyaka Upanishad II:V:18]

We will look more closely at divisibility in Book 2.

Prime Numbers

In Exercise 9c we may have noticed that some numbers only have one pair of factors. For example, $7 = 7 \times 1$ and there are no other numbers which multiply together to give 7. Such numbers are called primes or prime numbers.

Prime numbers are only divisible by one and themselves.

It was said that the number one cannot divide but in mathematics we pretend that the one can divide and be divided.

The first few prime numbers are 1, 2, 3, 5, 7, 11, 13, 17,...

The Sieve of Eratosthanes

Eratosthanes was a mathematician of ancient Greece who lived from 276 to 194 BC. He discovered a simple method for finding the prime numbers. A grid of ten by ten boxes is laid out and the numbers from 1 to 100 are written into the boxes.

The Vedic sutra used for this is,

By Elimination and Retention

Starting from 2 cross out every second number but not 2 itself. Move to 3 and cross out every third number but not 3 itself. Then with 4, cross out every fourth number but not 4 itself. Continue this crossing out of numbers up to 10. This will eliminate all the numbers which are not prime numbers.

1	2	3	4	5	6	7	8	9	10
11	12	13	14	15	16	17	18	19	20
21	22	23	24	25	26	27	28	29	30
31	32	33	34	35	36	37	38	39	40
41	42	43	44	45	46	47	48	49	50
51	52	53	54	55	56	57	58	59	60
61	62	63	64	65	66	67	68	69	70
71	72	73	74	75	76	77	78	79	80
81	82	83	84	85	86	87	88	89	90
91	92	93	94	95	96	97	98	99	100

Exercise 9d Make a sieve, like that of Eratosthanes, by making a one-hundred square as shown above. When all the numbers that are not primes have been crossed out make a list of all the prime numbers up to 100.

The Number Two

The number two stands for the two types of beings in the creation, good and evil.

> *There are two creations of beings in this world, the divine and the demonic.*

[Bhagavad Gita 16:6]

So the number two divides the creation into two types of beings. It also divides the numbers into two sorts, odd and even.

Odd and even numbers

There are two types of numbers according as to whether or not two is a factor. Numbers which have two as a factor are called **even**. Numbers which do not have two as a factor are called **odd**.

When two is divided into an odd number the remainder is always one which stands for the Absolute or God. For example, 2 divided into 7 is 3 remainder 1.

When two is divided into an even number the remainder is nought which is the unmanifest. For example, 2 into 6 is 3 remainder 0.

The even numbers are 2, 4, 6, 8, 10, 12, 14, and so on. In fact, any number which ends in a 2, 4, 6, 8 or 0 is even. An even number can be divided into two equal parts. For example, 48 can be divided by 2 into two lots of 24, because 24 + 24 = 48.

Exercise 9e Divide the following numbers by two:

1. 20	6. 16	11. 42	16. 32
2. 50	7. 26	12. 66	17. 54
3. 200	8. 62	13. 84	18. 72
4. 24	9. 48	14. 46	19. 98
5. 30	10. 64	15. 88	20. 102

The odd numbers are 1, 3, 5, 7, 9, 11, 13, 15, and so on. Any number which ends with a 1, 3, 5, 7 or 9 is an odd number. An odd number cannot be divided into two equal parts, for example, 9 = 4 + 5.

Exercise 9f Problems: Show your working

1. Write down the product of 3 and 8.

2. 15 is one factor of 30. What is the other factor?

3. Is 456 an even number or an odd number?

4. How many pairs of factors does 28 have?

5. What is the product of 4 and 15?

6. Write down all the even numbers between 20 and 34 inclusive.

7. Is 2561 an odd number or an even number?

8. Write down all the pairs of factors of 50.

9. What is the next even number after 36?

10. What is the previous odd number to 31?

11. How many even numbers are there from 22 to 36 inclusive?

12. Write down the product of 2, 3 and 4.

13. Think of two even numbers, write them down and multiply them together. Is your answer odd or even? Try this with another pair of even numbers.

14. Think of two numbers, one of which is odd and the other of which is even. Write them down and find their product. Is your answer odd or even? Try this with another two pairs?

15. Think of two odd numbers and multiply them together. Is your answer odd or even? Try this with another two pairs of odd numbers.

16. Think of two even numbers and add them together. Is your answer odd or even? Try this with another two pairs of even numbers.

17. Think of two numbers, one of which is odd and the other of which is even, and add them together. Is your answer odd or even? Try this with another two pairs?

18. Think of two odd numbers and add them together. Is your answer odd or even? Try this with another two pairs of even numbers.

19. In a certain street there are 98 houses with the odd-numbered houses on one side and the even-numbered houses on the other side. How many houses are there on each side?

20. On which side of an open book are the odd-numbered pages?

Multiples

Multiple means many and as soon as we have moved from one to two we are in the realm of many. In the play of number, if we take the number one many times we arrive at 2, 3, 4, 5, and so on. Similarly, if we take the number two many times we arrive at 4, 6, 8, 10, 12, and so on. These are all **multiples** of two.

A **multiple** of a number is that number multiplied by any number.

Exercise 9g

Write down the multiples of,

1. 3, from 3 to 30
2. 10, from 10 to 100
3. 5, from 5 to 60
4. 2, from 10 to 30
5. 7, from 14 to 42

6. 4, from 12 to 32
7. 8, from 48 to 96
8. 1, from 23 to 27
9. 9, from 9 to 45
10. 6 from 48 to 72

Write down the next two numbers in each pattern:

11. 4, 6, 8, 10, 12, __, __
12. 18, 21, 24, __, __
13. 35, 40, 45, __, __
14. 12, 18, 24, 30, __, __
15. 36, 45, 54, 63, __, __

16. 50, 100, 150, __, __
17. 40, 60, 80, 100, __, __
18. 30, 36, 42, __, __
19. 45, 40, 35, 30, __, __
20. 16, 32, 48, __, __

21. Write down a number which is a multiple of 4 and is more than 30.
22. Write down a number which is a multiple of 6 and a multiple of 4.
23. Write down a number which is a multiple of 2 and 3 and also 5.
24. Which number is a multiple of both 3 and 5 and is less than 20?
25. Which number is a multiple of both 3 and 5 and is between 20 and 40?
26. Which multiples of 5 are not multiples of 10 but are less than 40?
27. Write down a multiple of both 6 and 5 which is less than 60.
28. Write down three numbers which are multiples of both 2 and 3.
29. Which is the lowest number which is both a multiple of 2 and a multiple of 3?
30. Which number is the lowest multiple of both 4 and 6?

79

The Number Ten

The number ten is 1 with a nought next to it; the one stands for the Absolute and the nought for the unmanifest.

> *Ten people were going across the country to another land and they had to cross a river. The river was shallow but the currents were swift. They managed to cross the river, and after reaching the other shore, they wanted to make sure that no-one was drowned. Each of them lined the others up and found the total of nine only, for none of them would count himself. They were sorry and disturbed. A holy man was passing along the bank and seeing them miserable he asked the reason of their worries. They narrated their story. The holy man saw their difficulty and foolishness so he asked all of them to line up. With his stick he hit one and separated him from the others. The next one he hit twice, and then separated him. Likewise he hit the tenth man ten times and declared them ten and assured them that none was lost.*

> *This story is told to illustrate that the tenth is yourself. Tenth is the one with zero, which is unmanifest. One to nine are the numbers of manifestation, and at ten, the same Self which is one stands with unmanifest Nature by its side. Further on the same repetition of numbers occurs. The one at number ten embodies the nine manifestations within it. The creation starts with one and at ten it again stands as one with all the nine manifestations.*

> [Sri Sankaracarya]

Ten is one with a nought on the end and so when multiplying a number by ten the answer is the same but with a nought on the end.

Example: $34 \times 10 = 340$

The effect of multiplying a number by ten is to move every digit in that number one place to the left and a nought is added to the end. In the example of $34 \times 10 = 340$, the 3 is in the tens column and moves to the hundreds column, the 4 is in the units column and moves to the tens column. A nought is placed in the units column.

Exercise 9h Multiply the following numbers by ten:

1. 2	6. 16	11. 422	16. 3221
2. 5	7. 26	12. 660	17. 5409
3. 21	8. 62	13. 802	18. 7654
4. 24	9. 48	14. 406	19. 1298
5. 30	10. 64	15. 88	20. 1002

Dividing a number by ten is the opposite process. When the number to be divided ends in nought all we need to do is take a nought off.

Exercise 9i Divide the following numbers by ten:

1. 40	6. 340	11. 5670	16. 656470
2. 60	7. 260	12. 6650	17. 535400
3. 10	8. 530	13. 4500	18. 56000
4. 80	9. 600	14. 4000	19. 767580
5. 90	10. 790	15. 2340	20. 900080

When multiplying a decimal fraction by 10 the principle is the same. Each number is moved into the next column to the left. The effect of this is to move the decimal point one place to the right.

Examples $0.361 \times 10 = 3.61$
$0.4 \times 10 = 4$ (because 4.0 is the same as 4)
$1.2 \times 10 = 12$

Exercise 9j Multiply the following numbers by ten:

1. 0.75	6. 3.4	11. 32.1	16. 21.32
2. 0.46	7. 5.9	12. 41.6	17. 1.234
3. 0.11	8. 5.1	13. 56.7	18. 2.067
4. 0.49	9. 6.7	14. 90.0	19. 45.24
5. 0.88	10. 0.8	15. 56.8	20. 76.01

Summary

The basic numbers always remain one to nine and all extra numbers are only the product of these nine stages seen in different levels.

Just as the Absolute is inside everything so the number one is a factor of every number and every number is a factor of itself.

When numbers are multiplied together the answer is called the **product**.

Numbers which are multiplied together to give a product are called **factors** of that product.

All numbers have one and themselves as factors.

The number one is not a product and cannot be divided: it is indivisible.

A number which is a product is divisible by any one of its factors.

Prime numbers are only divisible by one and themselves.

The number two stands for the two types of beings in the creation, good and evil.

There are two types of numbers according as to whether or not two is a factor. Numbers which have two as a factor are called **even**. Numbers which do not have two as a factor are called **odd**.

When two is divided into an odd number the remainder is always one which stands for the Absolute or God.

When two is divided into an even number the remainder is always nought, which is the unmanifest.

An even number can be divided into two equal parts and an odd number cannot be divided into two equal parts.

A **multiple** of a number is that number multiplied by any number.

Chapter Ten Vinculums

Adding and subtracting ten and other numbers ending with nought.

When adding ten to a number all we need to do is add 1 to the ten's column.

Example: $347 + 10 = 357$

Exercise 10a Add 10 to each of these numbers: write answers only.

51. 3	7. 243	13. 698	19. 2313	25. 10292
2. 62	8. 531	14. 792	20. 4536	26. 34518
3. 80	9. 876	15. 599	21. 7970	27. 40060
4. 21	10. 534	16. 395	22. 4000	28. 78691
5. 46	11. 678	17. 192	23. 6791	29. 12995
6. 77	12. 300	18. 998	24. 4395	30. 99990

When subtracting ten from a number we just take 1 away from the digit in the ten's column.

Example: $326 - 10 = 316$

If 0 is in the ten's column then put a 9 in the ten's column and subtract 1 from the next column to the left, the hundreds column. Can you see why this works?

Example: $65702 - 10 = 65692$

When there is a nought in the ten's column and in adjacent columns to the left subtract 1 from the next number to the left and replace the noughts with nines. Can you see why this works?

Example: $340002 - 10 = 339992$

Exercise 10b   Subtract 10 from each of these numbers: write answers only.

1. 50	**7.** 646	**13.** 506	**19.** 4342	**25.** 3005
2. 34	**8.** 312	**14.** 701	**20.** 9786	**26.** 40501
3. 76	**9.** 657	**15.** 803	**21.** 5430	**27.** 34003
4. 12	**10.** 876	**16.** 709	**22.** 3401	**28.** 50000
5. 49	**11.** 680	**17.** 204	**23.** 5602	**29.** 65704
6. 97	**12.** 233	**18.** 102	**24.** 4301	**30.** 10009

Exercise 10c   Add 100 to each of these numbers by adding 1 to the digit in the hundreds column: write answers only.

1. 334	**7.** 987	**13.** 86	**19.** 3988	**25.** 87868
2. 456	**8.** 1672	**14.** 54	**20.** 6941	**26.** 54950
3. 129	**9.** 5874	**15.** 22	**21.** 7900	**27.** 12245
4. 786	**10.** 1000	**16.** 1779	**22.** 1921	**28.** 11011
5. 884	**11.** 2120	**17.** 1011	**23.** 5999	**29.** 76999
6. 920	**12.** 3657	**18.** 945	**24.** 5942	**30.** 99900

Exercise 10d   Subtract 100 from each of these numbers by taking 1 away from the digit in the hundreds column: write answers only.

1. 300	**7.** 654	**13.** 5463	**19.** 5087	**25.** 20000
2. 900	**8.** 121	**14.** 3411	**20.** 3021	**26.** 68796
3. 200	**9.** 140	**15.** 6766	**21.** 1043	**27.** 43251
4. 500	**10.** 579	**16.** 98765	**22.** 6081	**28.** 70000
5. 781	**11.** 644	**17.** 3022	**23.** 4011	**29.** 10099
6. 647	**12.** 101	**18.** 4010	**24.** 2059	**30.** 10000

Exercise 10e Add 20 to each of these numbers by adding 2 to the digit in the ten's column: write answers only.

1. 46	**7.** 66	**13.** 913	**19.** 5678	**25.** 80
2. 72	**8.** 79	**14.** 632	**20.** 9105	**26.** 90
3. 18	**9.** 4	**15.** 116	**21.** 6921	**27.** 390
4. 36	**10.** 512	**16.** 708	**22.** 5535	**28.** 480
5. 50	**11.** 623	**17.** 962	**23.** 1000	**29.** 196
6. 23	**12.** 747	**18.** 1124	**24.** 5340	**30.** 23295

Exercise 10f Mixed practice; write answers only:

1. 23 + 10	**11.** 146 + 10	**21.** 200 + 400	**31.** 6758 + 100
2. 45 − 10	**12.** 765 + 20	**22.** 234 + 100	**32.** 9812 − 100
3. 245 + 10	**13.** 453 − 10	**23.** 631 − 100	**33.** 3800 + 200
4. 18 − 10	**14.** 760 − 30	**24.** 542 − 200	**34.** 6520 − 300
5. 24 + 30	**15.** 555 − 20	**25.** 45 + 600	**35.** 1211 + 700
6. 82 − 20	**16.** 119 + 40	**26.** 387 + 300	**36.** 8788 − 700
7. 57 + 30	**17.** 830 + 70	**27.** 712 − 200	**37.** 4166 + 800
8. 12 + 60	**18.** 754 − 50	**28.** 412 + 600	**38.** 32 + 400
9. 88 − 40	**19.** 890 − 30	**29.** 987 − 900	**39.** 2986 − 900
10. 95 − 60	**20.** 774 + 30	**30.** 321 + 400	**40.** 1100 + 900

Vinculum numbers

Look at the following subtractions:-

$$9 = 10 - 1 = 1\overline{1}$$
$$8 = 10 - 2 = 1\overline{2}$$
$$7 = 10 - 3 = 1\overline{3}$$
$$6 = 10 - 4 = 1\overline{4}$$

In the first example, we have shown that 9 is the same as 10 − 1 and this may be written as one ten in the ten's column and 'take away' 1 in the units column. The second example shows that 8 is the same as 10 − 2 which may be written as one ten in the ten's column and 'take away' 2 in the units column.

A vinculum number is a 'take away' or minus number. Here is another example:

$$28 = 30 - 2 = 3\overline{2}$$

28 is the same as $30 - 2$. For short, we may write this as $3\overline{2}$, which is read as 'thirty vinculum two' or 'three vinculum two'. Notice that the 2 of $\overline{2}$ is the complement of 8.

The word 'vinculum' comes from the Latin word meaning 'chain' or 'bond'.
There are two sutras for changing a digit of a number into a vinculum number. These are *All from nine and the last from ten.* and *By one more than the one before.*

Exercise 10g Copy and complete the following:

1. $7 = 10 - 3 = 1\overline{1}$	11. $89 =$	$=$
2. $8 =$ $=$	12. $49 =$	$=$
3. $6 =$ $=$	13. $26 =$	$=$
4. $5 =$ $=$	14. $47 =$	$=$
5. $19 =$ $=$	15. $58 =$	$=$
6. $36 =$ $=$	16. $28 =$	$=$
7. $48 =$ $=$	17. $39 =$	$=$
8. $29 =$ $=$	18. $77 =$	$=$
9. $58 =$ $=$	19. $37 =$	$=$
10. $27 =$ $=$	20. $68 =$	$=$

Exercise 10h Copy and complete the following:

1. $1\overline{3} = 10 - 3 = 7$	11. $2\overline{1} =$	$=$
2. $2\overline{7} =$ $=$	12. $9\overline{1} =$	$=$
3. $3\overline{8} =$ $=$	13. $6\overline{4} =$	$=$
4. $4\overline{9} =$ $=$	14. $2\overline{3} =$	$=$
5. $5\overline{6} =$ $=$	15. $5\overline{8} =$	$=$
6. $7\overline{8} =$ $=$	16. $6\overline{8} =$	$=$
7. $9\overline{3} =$ $=$	17. $7\overline{3} =$	$=$
8. $8\overline{1} =$ $=$	18. $8\overline{3} =$	$=$
9. $9\overline{7} =$ $=$	19. $7\overline{1} =$	$=$
10. $8\overline{4} =$ $=$	20. $6\overline{3} =$	$=$

Whichever digit we wish to change into a vinculum number we need to find its complement. This is why the Nikhilam sutra is involved.

To change the units digit into a vinculum number, increase the tens digit by 1 and put down the complement of the units digit as the vinculum number.

Example: $47 = 5\bar{3}$

One more than 4 is 5 and the complement of 7 is 3.

Exercise 10i Change each units digit into a vinculum number.

1. 27	7. 16	13. 26	19. 46	25. 55
2. 39	8. 26	14. 48	20. 87	26. 39
3. 28	9. 77	15. 56	21. 59	27. 57
4. 17	10. 88	16. 25	22. 19	28. 29
5. 79	11. 49	17. 47	23. 69	29. 38
6. 18	12. 89	18. 37	24. 66	30. 9

To change a number back into its ordinary form, write down the complement of the vinculum number and subtract 1 from the next digit to the left. The sutras for this are *All from nine and the last from ten* and *By one less than the one before*.

Example: $7\bar{5} = 65$

The complement of 5 is 5 and $7 - 1 = 6$.

Exercise 10j Change these numbers back to their ordinary form.

1. $4\bar{8}$	5. $9\bar{2}$	9. $4\bar{4}$	13. $7\bar{5}$	17. $8\bar{2}$
2. $2\bar{2}$	6. $4\bar{5}$	10. $5\bar{1}$	14. $3\bar{1}$	18. $7\bar{4}$
3. $1\bar{8}$	7. $5\bar{5}$	11. $3\bar{2}$	15. $4\bar{2}$	19. $8\bar{5}$
4. $5\bar{3}$	8. $5\bar{2}$	12. $5\bar{4}$	16. $6\bar{2}$	20. $9\bar{1}$

21. 6$\bar{5}$	**25.** 4$\bar{3}$	**29.** 5$\bar{8}$	**33.** 29$\bar{3}$	**37.** 45$\bar{2}$
22. 7$\bar{1}$	**26.** 3$\bar{4}$	**30.** 6$\bar{1}$	**34.** 77$\bar{5}$	**38.** 64$\bar{2}$
23. 3$\bar{5}$	**27.** 6$\bar{3}$	**31.** 7$\bar{2}$	**35.** 48$\bar{1}$	**39.** 39$\bar{4}$
24. 7$\bar{3}$	**28.** 8$\bar{4}$	**32.** 8$\bar{3}$	**36.** 16$\bar{4}$	**40.** 23$\bar{2}$

Vinculum numbers are really **deficiencies**. We came across deficiencies in Nikhilam multiplication.

To change a tens column digit into a vinculum we use exactly the same method. The digit is replaced by its complement and the digit to the left is increased by 1.

Example: 174 = 2$\bar{3}$4

The complement of 7 is 3 and 1 + 1 = 2

This is saying that one hundred, seven tens and four units is the same as two hundreds, minus three tens and four units.

Exercise 10k Change each tens digit into a vinculum number.

1. 381	**7.** 562	**13.** 5393	**19.** 184	**25.** 93
2. 278	**8.** 371	**14.** 1280	**20.** 2073	**26.** 84
3. 690	**9.** 2391	**15.** 4361	**21.** 3264	**27.** 74
4. 261	**10.** 1170	**16.** 4462	**22.** 2495	**28.** 91
5. 582	**11.** 3361	**17.** 1082	**23.** 282	**29.** 80
6. 493	**12.** 4382	**18.** 2073	**24.** 461	**30.** 90

To change a vinculum digit back into an ordinary number put down its complement and subtract 1 from the digit to the left.

Example: 6$\bar{2}$1 = 581

The complement of 2 is 8 and 6 – 1 = 5.

Exercise 10l Change each tens vinculum digit back into an ordinary number.

1. $4\bar{3}3$	7. $9\bar{1}8$	13. $12\bar{1}5$	19. $121\bar{2}1$	25. $2\bar{1}3$
2. $5\bar{2}1$	8. $8\bar{2}6$	14. $43\bar{1}1$	20. $55\bar{4}5$	26. $1\bar{4}5$
3. $7\bar{1}2$	9. $3\bar{2}4$	15. $87\bar{4}3$	21. $67\bar{4}6$	27. $1\bar{5}6$
4. $5\bar{5}7$	10. $4\bar{3}2$	16. $76\bar{2}9$	22. $654\bar{1}2$	28. $71\bar{2}3$
5. $3\bar{3}2$	11. $7\bar{2}3$	17. $54\bar{1}0$	23. $707\bar{2}4$	29. $67\bar{2}8$
6. $7\bar{3}6$	12. $8\bar{3}1$	18. $33\bar{3}2$	24. $544\bar{1}6$	30. $11\bar{1}1$

Vinculums may be used where the digits are too big. For example, $38 = 4\bar{2}$ and 8 is greater than 2. So it may be easier to use vinculum numbers for calculations.

Numbers may have more than one vinculum number.

Example: $3\bar{2}45\bar{1}2 = 284492$

For this we can deal with $3\bar{2}$ and $5\bar{1}$ within the number separately. $3\bar{2} = 28$ and $5\bar{1} = 49$.

Exercise 10m Change each vinculum digit back into an ordinary number.

1. $4\bar{1}3\bar{1}$	7. $2\bar{1}3\bar{1}$	13. $1\bar{2}4\bar{1}2$	19. $4\bar{4}33\bar{3}$	25. $2\bar{2}2\bar{2}22$
2. $5\bar{2}4\bar{3}$	8. $4\bar{3}2\bar{2}$	14. $24\bar{3}2\bar{4}$	20. $5\bar{1}23\bar{1}$	26. $4\bar{1}3\bar{1}31$
3. $1\bar{1}2\bar{4}$	9. $5\bar{1}5\bar{1}$	15. $21\bar{2}1\bar{1}$	21. $42\bar{3}2\bar{2}$	27. $301\bar{2}1\bar{1}$
4. $4\bar{4}1\bar{3}$	10. $4\bar{4}4\bar{4}$	16. $31\bar{4}5\bar{3}$	22. $505\bar{1}4\bar{3}$	28. $2\bar{4}1\bar{1}10$
5. $5\bar{1}4\bar{2}$	11. $3\bar{3}3\bar{3}$	17. $6\bar{5}3\bar{2}1$	23. $43\bar{1}1\bar{2}$	29. $6\bar{3}5\bar{5}5$
6. $6\bar{3}5\bar{4}$	12. $7\bar{1}5\bar{1}$	18. $5\bar{4}3\bar{2}2$	24. $3\bar{1}1\bar{1}11$	30. $1\bar{2}22\bar{3}$

To make the digits small we can change any of the digits in a number which are more than 5 into a vinculum number.

Example: $381149 = 4\bar{2}115\bar{1}$

Vedic Mathematics for Schools 1

Exercise 10n Copy the number down and draw a circle around any number which is more than 5. Change the circled digits into vinculum digits.

1. 382	**7.** 3728	**13.** 39218	**19.** 10816	**25.** 1726
2. 193	**8.** 1727	**14.** 48109	**20.** 32618	**26.** 348
3. 373	**9.** 2809	**15.** 37190	**21.** 28119	**27.** 29181
4. 229	**10.** 4645	**16.** 28106	**22.** 27361	**28.** 27384
5. 327	**11.** 3821	**17.** 27316	**23.** 49172	**29.** 22518
6. 406	**12.** 3518	**18.** 19382	**24.** 33829	**30.** 44609

Adding and subtracting vinculum numbers

Vinculum numbers may be added or subtracted just like ordinary numbers.

Examples:
$$\bar{4} + \bar{2} = \bar{6}$$
$$\bar{5} - \bar{2} = \bar{3}$$
$$12 + \bar{3} = 9$$

Exercise 10p Write answers only

1. $\bar{3} + \bar{2}$	**11.** $\bar{5} - \bar{3}$	**21.** $\bar{4} + \bar{5}$	**31.** $10 + \bar{5}$
2. $\bar{1} + \bar{1}$	**12.** $\bar{4} - \bar{1}$	**22.** $\bar{8} - \bar{4}$	**32.** $8 + \bar{2}$
3. $\bar{2} + \bar{2}$	**13.** $\bar{5} - 0$	**23.** $\bar{9} - \bar{3}$	**33.** $6 + \bar{1}$
4. $\bar{4} + \bar{3}$	**14.** $\bar{3} - \bar{2}$	**24.** $\bar{7} - \bar{4}$	**34.** $7 + \bar{5}$
5. $\bar{1} + \bar{2}$	**15.** $\bar{4} - \bar{2}$	**25.** $\bar{2} + \bar{6}$	**35.** $8 + \bar{4}$
6. $\bar{4} + \bar{2}$	**16.** $\bar{4} - \bar{1}$	**26.** $\bar{9} - \bar{5}$	**36.** $9 + \bar{4}$
7. $\bar{5} + \bar{1}$	**17.** $\bar{5} - \bar{2}$	**27.** $\bar{3} + \bar{4}$	**37.** $10 + \bar{9}$
8. $\bar{3} + \bar{3}$	**18.** $\bar{4} - 0$	**28.** $\bar{2} + \bar{7}$	**38.** $2 + \bar{2}$
9. $\bar{2} + \bar{4}$	**19.** $\bar{2} - \bar{2}$	**29.** $\bar{8} - \bar{8}$	**39.** $5 - \bar{3}$
10. $\bar{5} + \bar{3}$	**20.** $\bar{3} - \bar{1}$	**30.** $\bar{7} - \bar{6}$	**40.** $8 - \bar{5}$

Chapter Eleven   Algebra

Codes

Long ago, the seers of India used a number code. The nine numbers and the nought were sometimes represented by the letters of the Sanskrit alphabet. This code enabled the ancient writers of Sanskrit poetry to write long numbers as words and verses made up of letters. This was done to help with the learning of long lists of numbers and to convey secret messages.

A similar code can be made from the letters of the English alphabet. The chart below shows one such code:

$$1 = \text{b, p or ph}$$
$$2 = \text{c, q or ch}$$
$$3 = \text{d, r or sk}$$
$$4 = \text{f, s or sh}$$
$$5 = \text{g, t or th}$$
$$6 = \text{h, v or gh}$$
$$7 = \text{j, w or wh}$$
$$8 = \text{k, x or kn}$$
$$9 = \text{l, z or double letter}$$
$$0 = \text{m, n or ng}$$

The way the code works is as follows:

1. There is a choice of letters for each number as shown in the table above.

2. The vowels, a, e, i, o, u and the letter y do not stand for any number.

Examples:

fat = 45 (f = 4 and t = 5),
father = 453 (f = 4, th = 5 and r = 3),
long = 90,
Sarah = 436,
coat and hat = 250365

Exercise 11a Find the numbers represented by these words and phrases:

1. cat	**11.** courage	**21.** trouble and strife
2. log	**12.** ice-cream	**22.** Be quiet!
3. book	**13.** together	**23.** Pass the butter
4. elder	**14.** little	**24.** Decode this number.
5. wish	**15.** computer	**25.** The man in the moon
6. what	**16.** spirit	**26.** a lazy zulu
7. tent	**17.** oxygen	**27.** pay car tax
8. snake	**18.** Mother	**28.** Look who hits our chap.
9. London	**19.** space shuttle	**29.** Can you name many men in Monaco?
10. church	**20.** Rolls Royce	**30.** Feed this dog, for 'tis a rogue.

When making up a word from a number there is a choice. For example, suppose we want to make a word for the number 100. The first letter is b, p or ph; the second letter is m, n or ng and the last letter is also m, n or ng. It is useful to make up a table as follows:

1	0	0
b	m	m
p	n	n
ph	ng	ng

'be a man', 'pining', 'banging', 'phone me', are all words or phrases which stand for the number 100.

Exercise 11b Using the code make up a word or phrase for each of the following numbers:

1. 20	**6.** 53	**11.** 5	**16.** 745	**21.** 1234
2. 45	**7.** 77	**12.** 3	**17.** 299	**22.** 7930
3. 78	**8.** 43	**13.** 1	**18.** 454	**23.** 4000
4. 21	**9.** 27	**14.** 907	**19.** 830	**24.** 4216
5. 10	**10.** 90	**15.** 232	**20.** 1001	**25.** 53463

In Algebra, we use letters to represent numbers. A letter may stand for a particular number or for any number in general. If a letter is given a particular value then that value remains the same in the same piece of work. For example, if we say, "let $x = 1$", we do not mean that x must always have the value 1, but only in the particular example we are considering.

Example: If x is 4, what is the value of $x + 6$?

$$x + 6 = 4 + 6 = 10$$

Exercise 11c   If $x = 5$, find the value of the following:

1. $x + 2$	6. $x - 1$	11. $9 - x$	16. $x - 4 + 4$
2. $x + 5$	7. $x - 4$	12. $24 - x$	17. $x - 1 + 8$
3. $10 + x$	8. $x - 5$	13. $320 - x$	18. $2 + x + 7$
4. $19 + x$	9. $x - 0$	14. $5 - x$	19. $3 + x - 3$
5. $x + 95$	10. $1 + x - 2$	15. $10 - x + 3$	20. $10 + x - 15$

If $y = 2$ find the value of the following:

21. $4 + y$	26. $2 \times y$	31. $y + y$	36. $3 - y + 8$
22. $3 - y$	27. $7 \times y$	32. $y + 3 - y$	37. $9 \times y$
23. $2 + 2 + y$	28. $10 \div y$	33. $y + y + y$	38. $y \times y$
24. $6 - y$	29. $8 \times y$	34. $5 + y - 7$	39. $50 \times y$
25. $1 + 2 - y$	30. $8 \div y$	35. $4 + y + y$	40. $50 \div y$

When a letter standing for a number is preceded by a number the two are joined by multiplication. For example, $3y$ means $3 \times y$, or 'three lots of a number y'

Example: If x is 5, what is the value of $3x - 6$?

$$3x - 6 = 3 \times 5 - 6 = 15 - 6$$

93

Exercise 11d If $a = 3$, find the value of the following:

1. $2a$	**6.** $0a$	**11.** $100a$	**16.** $3a + 6a$
2. $4a$	**7.** $5a$	**12.** $6a$	**17.** $2a + 4a$
3. $8a$	**8.** $3a$	**13.** $11a$	**18.** $7a + 1a$
4. $7a$	**9.** $9a$	**14.** $20a$	**19.** $9a + 5a$
5. $1a$	**10.** $10a$	**15.** $12a$	**20.** $10a - 6a$

If $b = 2$ find the value of the following:

21. $4b$	**26.** $6b$	**31.** $11b$	**36.** $2b + 7b$
22. $7b$	**27.** $3b$	**32.** $0b$	**37.** $13b$
23. $9b$	**28.** $10b$	**33.** $25b$	**38.** $3b + 5b$
24. $2b$	**29.** $1b$	**34.** $12b$	**39.** $8b + 6b$
25. $5b$	**30.** $8b$	**35.** $30b$	**40.** $7b + 7b$

Exercise 11e Find the value of the following:

1. $a = 2,\ 4a =$	**6.** $a = 4,\ 4a =$	**11.** $a = 6,\ 100a =$
2. $a = 4,\ 2a =$	**7.** $a = 5,\ 4a =$	**12.** $a = 1,\ 17a =$
3. $a = 10,\ 3a =$	**8.** $a = 9,\ 11a =$	**13.** $a = 8,\ 8a =$
4. $a = 6,\ 7a =$	**9.** $a = 2,\ 9a =$	**14.** $a = 15,\ 2a =$
5. $a = 1,\ 8a =$	**10.** $a = 12,\ 6a =$	**15.** $a = 9,\ 6a =$

If $a = 2$, $b = 3$ and $c = 4$, find the value of the following:

16. $a + b$	**21.** $a + b + c$	**26.** $5b$	**31.** $5b + a$
17. $b + c$	**22.** $a + b - c$	**27.** $2a + b$	**32.** $3a + 2b$
18. $a + c$	**23.** $c - a + b$	**28.** $3b + c$	**33.** $6c + 2a$
19. $c - a$	**24.** $c + b - a$	**29.** $6a - c$	**34.** $2c - 2a$
20. $b - a$	**25.** $b - a + c$	**30.** $4c + b$	**35.** $9b - 2a - c$

Equations

An equation is a sentence which expresses equality. In mathematics an equation has an equals sign.

Here are some examples of equations:

$2 + 4 = 6$,   Two plus four equals six;
$17 - 7 = 9 + 1$,   Seventeen minus seven equals nine plus one;
$x + x = 2x$, x plus x equals two times x;

An equation is like a balance. Both sides must be equal.

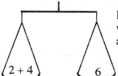

In Mathematics, we write this 'balance' as $2 + 4 = 6$.

Exercise 11f Find the numbers which must be added to the left-hand side to make each balance equal. Write answers only.

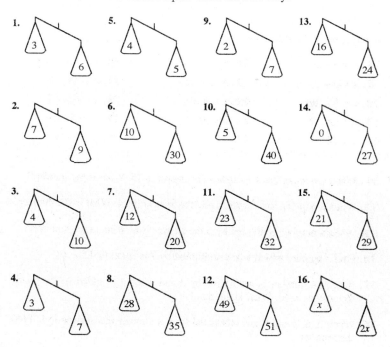

1. 3 / 6
2. 7 / 9
3. 4 / 10
4. 3 / 7
5. 4 / 5
6. 10 / 30
7. 12 / 20
8. 28 / 35
9. 2 / 7
10. 5 / 40
11. 23 / 32
12. 49 / 51
13. 16 / 24
14. 0 / 27
15. 21 / 29
16. x / $2x$

Solving Equations

Solving an equation means finding the hidden number. The hidden number is called the solution.

Example: $\quad x = 3 + 5$
$\quad\underline{x = 8}\ $ is the solution

Exercise 11g Solve these equations:

1. $x = 12 + 6$	**6.** $p = 400 - 199$	**11.** $e = 2 \times 15$
2. $a = 34 - 17$	**7.** $z = 32 \div 8$	**12.** $h = 16 - 7 + 8$
3. $b = 100 \div 2$	**8.** $a = 96 + 4$	**13.** $m = 9 - 4 + 1$
4. $y = 2 \times 26$	**9.** $c = 4 \times 4 \times 2$	**14.** $n = 10 \div 2$
5. $x = 25 \times 3$	**10.** $d = 17 - 16$	**15.** $t = 5 \times 5 \times 5$

If $b = 3$, solve the following:

16. $x = b$	**21.** $x = 4 + b$	**26.** $x = 10b - 28$
17. $x = b + 2$	**22.** $x = 3 - b$	**27.** $x = 7b + 14$
18. $x = b - 1$	**23.** $x = b \times b$	**28.** $x = 6b - 7$
19. $x = 2b$	**24.** $x = 3b$	**29.** $x = 15 + 5b$
20. $x = 14 + b$	**25.** $x = 2b - 5$	**30.** $x = b \times b \times b$

31. When a number has two added the answer is 15. What is the number?

32. When a number has 3 taken away the answer is 24. What is the number?

33. When a number is divided by 5 the answer is 6. What is the number?

34. Find a number which when multiplied by 7 is equal to 42.

35. A certain number is multiplied by 2 and when 4 is added to the result the answer is 16. What is the number?

36. When 2, 6, 4 and 8 are subtracted from a number the answer is 1. Find the number.

An equation has two sides, a left-hand side and a right-hand side. The left-hand side is everything that is to the left of the equals sign and the right-hand side is everything that is to the right of the equals sign.

When the letter is not by itself we have to move the numbers until the letter is by itself.

Example: $x - 2 = 6$

In this example the left-hand side is $x - 2$ and so x is not by itself; it has a minus two after it. To solve this equation we need to obtain $x = $ 'something'. To do this we use a sutra which says *Paravartya Yojayet*, which means,

Transpose and Adjust.

'Transpose' here means to move a number from one side of the equation to the other. 'Adjust' means to change the sign to the opposite.

$$\begin{array}{c} \text{We adjust,} \qquad - \text{ to } + \\ + \text{ to } - \\ \times \text{ to } \div \\ \div \text{ to } \times \end{array}$$

In the example, $x - 2 = 6$, to obtain x by itself we move the $- 2$ from the left-hand side to the right-hand side and change the sign from a minus to a plus.

$$\begin{array}{rl} \text{Example:} & x - 2 = 6 \\ & x \quad\;\; = 6 + 2 \\ & \underline{x \;\; = 8} \end{array}$$

Exercise 11h Solve these equations. Keep the equal signs in line.

1. $x + 1 = 4$

2. $x + 2 = 5$

3. $x + 7 = 14$

4. $x + 8 = 20$

5. $x + 3 = 3$

6. $x - 2 = 0$

7. $x - 7 = 6$

8. $x - 3 = 9$

9. $x - 5 = 20$

10. $x - 15 = 80$

11. $x + 4 = 4$

12. $x - 6 = 28$

13. $x - 1 = 99$

14. $x + 37 = 38$

15. $x - 200 = 150$

Example: $5 + x = 24$
             $x = 24 - 5$
             $x = 19$

---

16. $2 + x = 5$ **21.** $10 + x = 22$ **26.** $61 + x = 70$

17. $6 + x = 8$ **22.** $9 + x = 18$ **27.** $35 + x = 47$

18. $4 + x = 5$ **23.** $12 + x = 16$ **28.** $251 + x = 259$

19. $16 + x = 16$ **24.** $15 + x = 25$ **29.** $68 + x = 99$

20. $0 + x = 7$ **25.** $20 + x = 50$ **30.** $74 + x = 275$

When the unknown number is on the right-hand side of the equation we can transpose numbers the other way. Always leave your answer with the letter on the left.

Example: $4 = x - 12$
             $4 + 12 = x$ -12 is transposed from the right to
             $16 = x$ the left-hand side and the sign
             $x = 16$ changes from $-$ to $+$.

Exercise 11i Solve these equations. Keep the equal signs in line.

1. $3 = x + 3$ **11.** $34 = x - 30$ **21.** $45 = x + 12$

2. $7 = x + 2$ **12.** $4 = x - 3$ **22.** $67 = x - 3$

3. $15 = x + 10$ **13.** $5 = x - 10$ **23.** $21 = x - 8$

4. $23 = x + 5$ **14.** $12 = x - 1$ **24.** $87 = x + 27$

5. $27 = x + 16$ **15.** $0 = x - 6$ **25.** $354 = x - 646$

6. $12 = x + 7$ **16.** $2 = x - 4$ **26.** $53 = x + 2$

7. $17 = x + 5$ **17.** $1 = x - 7$ **27.** $16 = x - 14$

8. $25 = x + 12$ **18.** $33 = x - 20$ **28.** $111 = x - 9$

9. $33 = x + 14$ **19.** $51 = x - 4$ **29.** $64 = x + 63$

10. $67 = x + 22$ **20.** $30 = x - 56$ **30.** $218 = x - 121$

Example:
$$12 = 3 + x$$
$$12 - 3 = \quad x$$
$$9 = \quad x$$
$$\underline{x = 9}$$

Exercise 11j Solve these equations. Keep the equal signs in line.

1. $11 = 3 + x$	**6.** $24 = 18 + x$	**11.** $27 = 5 + x$
2. $40 = 1 + x$	**7.** $45 = 35 + x$	**12.** $48 = 24 + x$
3. $20 = 15 + x$	**8.** $21 = 19 + x$	**13.** $100 = 86 + x$
4. $16 = 11 + x$	**9.** $56 = 34 + x$	**14.** $1000 = 378 + x$
5. $8 = 8 + x$	**10.** $70 = 55 + x$	**15.** $927 = 126 + x$

When there is a number multiplying a letter standing for a number, such as $6x$, we can change the sign to divides and put the number on the other side of the equation.

$6p = 18$	$14 = 7q$
$p = 18 \div 6$	$14 \div 7 = q$
$\underline{p = 3}$	$2 = q$
	$\underline{q = 2}$

Exercise 11k Solve:

1. $2a = 6$	**9.** $4q = 0$	**17.** $30 = 3y$	**25.** $6 = 3p$
2. $3b = 12$	**10.** $6x = 24$	**18.** $7 = 1a$	**26.** $24 = 8x$
3. $5r = 5$	**11.** $10x = 20$	**19.** $12 = 6b$	**27.** $36 = 9z$
4. $9s = 18$	**12.** $12b = 48$	**20.** $54 = 9c$	**28.** $32 = 4t$
5. $4x = 12$	**13.** $9a = 108$	**21.** $96 = 12d$	**29.** $16 = 2b$
6. $3y = 6$	**14.** $7d = 56$	**22.** $64 = 8c$	**30.** $72 = 6w$
7. $7t = 49$	**15.** $11c = 99$	**23.** $9 = 3g$	**31.** $72 = 8p$
8. $5p = 25$	**16.** $22 = 2x$	**24.** $15 = 5n$	**32.** $55 = 55k$

Simplifying

We can simplify expressions by collecting terms together which are like one another.

Simplify $a + 2a + a + 3a + a$ Remember that $a = 1a$

$$a + 2a + a + 3a + a = 8a$$

Simplify $6a - 2a + 4a$

$$6a - 2a + 4a = 8a$$

Exercise 11l Simplify by collecting terms:

1. $a + 3a$
2. $2b + 3b$
3. $c + 5c$
4. $2h + 5h$
5. $9s + 3s$
6. $12p + p$
7. $40t + 5t$
8. $4q + 8q$
9. $17f + 17f$
10. $21m + 16m$

11. $a + 2a + 5a$
12. $p + p + 3p$
13. $2g + g + 4g$
14. $7y + y + 2y$
15. $2b + 3b + 4b$
16. $n + n + n + n$
17. $5x + 3x + x$
18. $8d + 3d + d$
19. $4e + 2e + 5e$
20. $7k + 2k + k$

21. $x + 4x + x + 3x$
22. $2h + 2h + 2h$
23. $a + 2a + 3a + 4a$
24. $m + m + m + m + m$
25. $3p + 2p + p + 5p$
26. $2z + 7z + 4z + z$
27. $6b + b + b + b + b$
28. $3y + 3y + 3y + 3y$
29. $c + 8c + 4c + 3c$
30. $10x + 20x + 70x$

31. $9a - 3a$
32. $15x - 7x$
33. $20h - 3h$
34. $8c - 8c$
35. $18d - 12d$
36. $25b - 15b$
37. $32m - 4m$

38. $4x + 5x - 6x$
39. $7y - 5y + 3y$
40. $2w + 4w - w$
41. $9d - d + 6d$
42. $a + 7a - 8a$
43. $6s + 4s - 6s$
44. $f + 4f - 4f$

45. $3k - k + k - k + k$
46. $4n + 3n - 3n + 2n$
47. $10x - 5x - 4x + x$
48. $v - v + 2v - 2v + v$
49. $3p + 17p - 19p$
50. $26t - 18t - 2t + 3t$
51. $8z - 3z + 32z - z$

ANSWERS

Vedic Mathematics for Schools   Book 1

Answers

Chapter One   Revision of Number

Exercise 1a

1. 5 units	**6.** 5 hundreds	**11.** 5 thousands	**16.** 5 hundreds
2. 5 units	**7.** 5 tens	**12.** 5 units	**17.** 5 tens
3. 5 tens	**8.** 5 units	**13.** 5 hundreds	**18.** 5 ten thousands
4. 5 units	**9.** 5 hundreds	**14.** 5 thousands	**19.** 5 thousands
5. 5 tens	**10.** 5 hundreds	**15.** 5 ten thousands	**20.** 5 hundreds

Exercise 1b

A   Thirty-five

B   Seventy-two

C   Sixty-one

D   Three hundred and forty-five

E   Six hundred and seven

F   Three hundred and ninety-two

G   One thousand four hundred and twenty-six

H   Five thousand seven hundred and eighty-nine

I   Four thousand two hundred and forty-five

J   Five thousand six hundred

K   Nine thousand and three

L   One thousand three hundred and twenty eight

Exercise 1c

A three hundred and fifty-four

B Four hundred and seventeen

C Nine hundred and eighty

D Six thousand, five hundred and three

E Nine thousand, eight hundred and seventy-six

K Fifty-six thousand two hundred and fourteen

L Ninety-nine thousand, nine hundred and ninety-nine

M One hundred and thirteen thousand, five hundred and six

N Three hundred and twelve thousand, five hundred and forty-six

F Five thousand and thiry-two

G Three thousand two hundred and one

H Seven thousand eight hundred and seventy-nine

I One thousand six hundred and fifty-four

J Eleven thousand three hun.. ' and forty-seven

O Two hundred and thirty-six thousand and one

P Three million, two hundred and sixty-five thousand and eighty-seven

Q Six million, two hundred and si thousand, four hundred and sixty-one

Exercise 1d Write the following numbers in words:

1. Twelve
2. Thirty-eight
3. Forty-two
4. Fifty-seven
5. Eighty-seven
6. Fifty-four
7. Twenty-five
8. Seventy-seven
9. Ninety-nine
10. One hundred and one

11. Two hundred and forty-three
12. Five hundred and six
13. Seven hundred and eighty-one
14. One hundred and fifty-four
15. Four hundred and fifty-six
16. Six hundred and seventy
17. Four hundred and five
18. Nine hundred and twenty
19. Five hundred and seventy-one
20. Six hundred and sixty-five

21. Five thousand, four hundred and sixty-three

22. Seven thousand, six hundred and fifty-eight

23. Six thousand

24. Seven thousand and two

25. Four thousand and fifty-six

26. Four thousand, two hundred and five

27. Two thousand, eight hundred and three

28. Eight thousand, nine hundred and thirty

29. One thousand, four hundred and fifty-five

30. Nine thousand, eight hundred and ninety-seven

---

31. Seventy-six thousand, eight hundred and fifty-two

32. Forty thousand and six

33. Fifty-seven thousand and three

34. Fifty thousand, three hundred and four

35. Eighty-nine thousand, six hundred and fifty four

36. Eight thousand, six hundred

37. Forty-two thousand

38. Four hundred and fifty-one thousand and three

39. Seven hundred and sixty-eight thousand, three hundred and seven

40. Eight million, nine hundred and twenty thousand and forty-three

Exercise 1e

1. 19	11. 600	21. 920	31. 1200
2. 42	12. 109	22. 721	32. 3042
3. 58	13. 250	23. 437	33. 208
4. 73	14. 560	24. 314	34. 4600
5. 95	15. 301	25. 648	35. 9029
6. 68	16. 809	26. 273	36. 10400
7. 31	17. 500	27. 366	37. 25000
8. 82	18. 111	28. 1500	38. 900000
9. 12	19. 614	29. 8029	39. 6000000
10. 29	20. 930	30. 6012	40. 4332000

Exercise 1f

1. 6, 7	6. 39, 41	11. 60, 50	16. 125, 130
2. 10, 12	7. 28, 31	12. 52, 58	17. 40, 48
3. 9, 11	8. 37, 41	13. 175, 200	18. 63, 72
4. 18, 21	9. 50, 60	14. 100, 120	19. 15, 21
5. 28, 30	10. 72, 84	15. 21, 19	20. 62, 126

Exercise 1g

1. 11	11. 6	21. 24	31. 66
2. 14	12. 14	22. 23	32. 67
3. 27	13. 25	23. 56	33. 14
4. 24	14. 61	24. 55	34. 15
5. 16	15. 67	25. 62	35. 68
6. 13	16. 27	26. 61	36. 69
7. 15	17. 36	27. 76	37. 124
8. 17	18. 14	28. 75	38. 125
9. 18	19. 30	29. 44	39. 346
10. 26	20. 21	30. 43	40. 347

Exercise 1h

1. 69	6. 161	11. 1074	16. 298	21. 11372	26. 10666
2. 95	7. 91	12. 568	17. 999	22. 10902	27. 9421
3. 106	8. 106	13. 254	18. 700	23. 9209	28. 5336
4. 54	9. 127	14. 1154	19. 1093	24. 4456	29. 8472
5. 64	10. 102	15. 521	20. 925	25. 6349	30. 19216

Exercise 1i

1. 31	4. 72	7. 72	10. 26	13. 362
2. 51	5. 101	8. 91	11. 163	14. 254
3. 61	6. 30	9. 36	12. 474	15. 571

Exercise 1j

1. 12	6. 62	11. 135	16. 621	21. 6352	26. 4423
2. 21	7. 30	12. 221	17. 242	22. 2201	27. 4001
3. 24	8. 29	13. 544	18. 851	23. 4316	28. 3201
4. 11	9. 44	14. 475	19. 611	24. 6110	29. 6721
5. 32	10. 22	15. 199	20. 201	25. 4797	30. 74514

Exercise 1k

1. 13	4. 58	7. 57	10. 3	13. 295
2. 32	5. 87	8. 79	11. 146	14. 244
3. 48	6. 18	9. 14	12. 459	15. 494

Exercise 1l

	6	18	0	56
	20	90	40	1
A	24	48	10	30
	12	18	27	72
	40	28	25	100
	9	9	14	0
	0	0	45	12
B	40	24	40	81
	36	80	8	28
	36	6	36	30
	3	0	0	4
	0	24	30	64
C	5	49	36	54
	21	60	35	0
	18	4	16	0
	8	0	6	12
	27	50	45	12
D	70	0	56	10
	48	32	72	21
	56	18	50	54
	42	120	0	24
	55	88	96	16
E	0	15	24	44
	11	18	48	60
	63	84	77	30

Exercise 1m

	4	1	8	3
	6	8	4	2
A	8	9	7	3
	4	6	3	4
	9	4	4	8
	2	1	7	5
	3	5	7	0
B	1	1	6	2
	6	5	7	3
	2	2	5	7

C			
4	4	10	9
5	5	9	3
8	10	4	7
9	3	0	9
7	5	6	6

D			
10	2	3	8
5	7	6	8
2	2	1	7
5	8	6	9
5	7	9	10

E			
2	9	5	4
6	9	6	5
7	6	2	8
5	3	12	9
7	1	9	20

Chapter Two   Multiplication by Nikhilam

Exercise 2a

1. 13	7. 36	13. 97	19. 8889	25. 4996600
2. 06	8. 72	14. 8660	20. 61270	26. 876020
3. 64	9. 56	15. 6436	21. 72537	27. 546399
4. 58	10. 27	16. 1996	22. 645400	28. 635280
5. 12	11. 126	17. 69540	23. 29397	29. 7241593
6. 25	12. 574	18. 1362	24. 00008	30. 3333333

Exercise 2b

1. 72	3. 54	5. 63	7. 45	9. 81
2. 64	4. 56	6. 48	8. 49	10. 36

Exercise 2c

1. 9212	7. 9604	13. 9108	19. 9306	25. 9504
2. 8918	8. 9207	14. 9114	20. 9016	26. 7546
3. 8924	9. 9506	15. 9216	21. 9118	27. 9120
4. 9312	10. 9405	16. 9215	22. 8827	28. 8928
5. 9801	11. 9009	17. 8832	23. 8448	29. 8624
6. 9702	12. 9408	18. 9310	24. 7938	30. 8633

Exercise2d

1. 992012	11. 858141	21. 941168
2. 983060	12. 871254	22. 988027
3. 871128	13. 991008	23. 984048
4. 893312	14. 990021	24. 979038
5. 998001	15. 990025	25. 815184
6. 681318	16. 980100	26. 873250
7. 993012	17. 896400	27. 981070
8. 986049	18. 978121	28. 969168
9. 988035	19. 978021	29. 686624
10. 987042	20. 963070	30. 598800

Exercise2e

1. 132	3. 154	5. 143	7. 165	9. 121
2. 144	4. 156	6. 168	8. 169	10 150

Exercise2f

1. 10812	11. 11445	21. 10918
2. 11118	12. 11128	22. 11227
3. 11124	13. 10908	23. 11648
4. 10712	14. 10914	24. 12138
5. 10201	15. 10816	25. 11845
6. 10302	16. 11550	26. 12480
7. 10404	17. 11232	27. 11555
8. 10807	18. 11555	28. 12463
9. 10506	19. 10706	29. 13668
10. 10920	20. 11016	30. 19998

Exercise2g

1. 9603	8. 8645	15. 8556	22. 6336
2. 9021	9. 8835	16. 8930	23. 7154
3. 9409	10. 8184	17. 8544	24. 7663
4. 8820	11. 8463	18. 8910	25. 6958
5. 8742	12. 8280	19. 9024	26. 8352
6. 8736	13. 8360	20. 9025	27. 6076
7. 8455	14. 7524	21. 8342	28. 5742

Exercise2h

1. 11021	8. 11336	15. 10404	22. 10609
2. 11330	9. 10920	16. 10506	23. 11016
3. 10712	10. 11025	17. 11128	24. 12096
4. 11130	11. 11766	18. 11440	25. 12566
5. 11660	12. 11445	19. 11865	26. 13770
6. 11340	13. 11872	20. 12360	27. 14847
7. 11118	14. 10914	21. 12064	28. 12036

Exercise2i

1. 9603	11. 11227	21. 1012027
2. 9120	12. 10807	22. 1025046
3. 9016	13. 995006	23. 1020096
4. 8827	14. 986045	24. 1035096
5. 7372	15. 989030	25. 99860024
6. 8550	16. 998001	26. 96720975
7. 10506	17. 989028	27. 98550286
8. 10920	18. 877242	28. 81317460
9. 10918	19. 1005006	29. 76874622
10. 11556	20. 1011028	30. 87963603

Exercise2j

1. 9016	11. 11772	21. 1012027
2. 9603	12. 8556	22. 97840428
3. 10908	13. 995006	23. 86723975
4. 9025	14. 990024	24. 98950404
5. 11817	15. 1006008	25. 1117230
6. 13464	16. 1013040	26. 8536
7. 8924	17. 1010016	27. 9999100014
8. 11021	18. 1015050	28. 634365
9. 8928	19. 99940008	29. 1037070
10. 11235	20. 11556	30. 9999800001

Chapter Three - Division

Exercise 3a

1. 9	7. 13	13. 7	19. 3011	25. 601
2. 42	8. 110	14. 7	20. 412	26. 602
3. 12	9. 112	15. 8	21. 511	27. 713
4. 11	10. 511	16. 8	22. 32241	28. 812
5. 24	11. 3412	17. 9	23. 2110	29. 710
6. 14	12. 2133	18. 9	24. 32401	30. 311

Exercise 3b

1. 1/1	7. 5/1	13. 2/1	19. 4/1	25. 8/1
2. 2/1	8. 3/1	14. 0/3	20. 5/6	26. 12/2
3. 2/1	9. 5/3	15. 0/1	21. 9/2	27. 8/1
4. 3/1	10. 4/2	16. 6/1	22. 8/5	28. 11/1
5. 5/1	11. 10/1	17. 2/2	23. 10/2	29. 0/2
6. 8/1	12. 0/2	18. 0/1	24. 5/4	30. 9/2

Exercise 3c Division with remainders

1. 122/2	7. 1074/1	13. 31/3	19. 2150/1	25. 205
2. 422/1	8. 411/3	14. 420/4	20. 3558/2	26. 644/3
3. 1208/1	9. 1413/3	15. 884/3	21. 6492/1	27. 2930
4. 2073/2	10. 503/5	16. 326/5	22. 32266	28. 4188/1
5. 2443/1	11. 1775/1	17. 2413/2	23. 10755/2	29. 1311/3
6. 1032/1	12. 2242/2	18. 684/2	24. 45455	30. 292/4

Exercise 3d Dividing by nine

1. 12/3	7. 13/6	13. 45/7	19. 124/5	25. 1233/5
2. 13/4	8. 11/8	14. 55/8	20. 137/8	26. 1356/7
3. 15/7	9. 15/8	15. 68/8	21. 234/5	27. 4678/8
4. 13/5	10. 22/3	16. 67/8	22. 346/7	28. 1336/7
5. 16/6	11. 23/4	17. 25/7	23. 356/6	29. 2257/8
6. 11/4	12. 35/6	18. 57/7	24. 455/7	30. 8888/8

Exercise 3e Nikhilam division

1. 2/6	6. 2/6	11. 2/7	16. 155/6
2. 3/7	7. 2/3	12. 6/7	17. 266/7
3. 12/5	8. 2/6	13. 4/6	18. 444/4
4. 12/6	9. 4/4	14. 3/4	19. 258/8
5. 1/6	10. 3/6	15. 11/1	20. 1/9 = 2/0

Exercise 3f Nikhilam division

1. 1/25	**6.** 2/09	**11.** 1/78	**16.** 6/25
2. 1/38	**7.** 2/37	**12.** 2/18	**17.** 2/54
3. 1/30	**8.** 1/33	**13.** 1/36	**18.** 3/37
4. 1/63	**9.** 1/53	**14.** 5/41	**19.** 2/80
5. 1/70	**10.** 2/73	**15.** 1/45	**20.** 1/84

Exercise 3g

1. 1/69	**6.** 2/69	**11.** 7/91	**16.** 2/28
2. 1/57	**7.** 4/50	**12.** 3/70	**17.** 3/84
3. 2/68	**8.** 2/63	**13.** 1/65	**18.** 2/84
4. 2/37	**9.** 3/77	**14.** 2/72	**19.** 2/83
5. 3/57	**10.** 2/68	**15.** 4/94	**20.** 4/83

Exercise 3h Nikhilam division with any base

1. 1/33	**6.** 1/56	**11.** 1/4132	**16.** 1/446
2. 1/35	**7.** 1/332	**12.** 1/422	**17.** 1/28
3. 1/49	**8.** 1/368	**13.** 1/336	**18.** 1/261
4. 1/28	**9.** 1/3157	**14.** 1/662	
5. 1/61	**10.** 1/4196	**15.** 1/305	

Exercise 3i Further practice with different bases

1. 2/36	**6.** 1/07	**11.** 1/2625	**16.** 1/335
2. 3/39	**7.** 1/175	**12.** 3/789	**17.** 1/242
3. 1/67	**8.** 2/433	**13.** 4/165	**18.** 1/436
4. 2/65	**9.** 2/2148	**14.** 1/754	
5. 1/05	**10.** 1/2433	**15.** 1/645	

Chapter Four - Digital Roots

Exercise 4a

1. 5	**9.** 6	**17.** 5	**25.** 8	**33.** 4
2. 8	**10.** 2	**18.** 3	**26.** 6	**34.** 9
3. 3	**11.** 3	**19.** 1	**27.** 9	**35.** 2
4. 8	**12.** 5	**20.** 1	**28.** 2	**36.** 2
5. 6	**13.** 6	**21.** 6	**29.** 8	**37.** 3
6. 7	**14.** 5	**22.** 2	**30.** 4	**38.** 3
7. 9	**15.** 5	**23.** 5	**31.** 9	**39.** 8
8. 8	**16.** 5	**24.** 4	**32.** 1	**40.** 9

Exercise 4b

1. 3	**9.** 6	**17.** 7	**25.** 7	**33.** 9
2. 6	**10.** 2	**18.** 6	**26.** 7	**34.** 9
3. 7	**11.** 6	**19.** 2	**27.** 5	**35.** 3
4. 2	**12.** 8	**20.** 3	**28.** 6	**36.** 1
5. 5	**13.** 4	**21.** 1	**29.** 1	**37.** 7
6. 2	**14.** 3	**22.** 4	**30.** 6	**38.** 3
7. 1	**15.** 3	**23.** 8	**31.** 9	**39.** 9
8. 6	**16.** 3	**24.** 8	**32.** 4	**40.** 3

Chapter Five   Vertically and Crosswise

Exercise 5a

1. 372	**11.** 483	**21.** 364	**31.** 529
2. 231	**12.** 208	**22.** 476	**32.** 1456
3. 156	**13.** 247	**23.** 2091	**33.** 1216
4. 308	**14.** 378	**24.** 675	**34.** 1638
5. 416	**15.** 512	**25.** 546	**35.** 3763
6. 154	**16.** 273	**26.** 735	**36.** 5628
7. 420	**17.** 420	**27.** 848	**37.** 6825
8. 690	**18.** 312	**28.** 576	**38.** 110
9. 132	**19.** 836	**29.** 1003	**39.** 374
10. 144	**20.** 770	**30.** 630	**40.** 286

Exercise 5b

1. 1472	**5.** £848	**9.** 1113	**13.** 1785	**17.** 960
2. 1104	**6.** 238	**10.** 336	**14.** 744	**18.** 350
3. 4452	**7.** 288	**11.** £30.72	**15.** 1344	
4. 1176	**8.** 608	**12.** £952	**16.** 456	

Exercise 5c

1. 48	**9.** 72	**17.** 900	**25.** 18066	**33.** 61023
2. 64	**10.** 52	**18.** 1082	**26.** 27060	**34.** 160060
3. 88	**11.** 246	**19.** 416	**27.** 5478	**35.** 306612
4. 75	**12.** 806	**20.** 1020	**28.** 20136	**36.** 187320
5. 123	**13.** 1536	**21.** 6482	**29.** 15964	**37.** 580779
6. 84	**14.** 666	**22.** 16050	**30.** 4356	**38.** 302701
7. 93	**15.** 646	**23.** 7323	**31.** 20046	**39.** 525928
8. 68	**16.** 420	**24.** 4092	**32.** 48638	**40.** 788904

Exercise 5d

1. 402028	4. 922206	7. 562204	10. 34817848
2. 226464	5. 453612	8. 692160	11. 1111104
3. 12004542	6. 2615060	9. 2815623	12. 999999

Exercise 5e Vertically and crosswise for three-digit by three-digit numbers

1. 14883	7. 91663	13. 35370	19. 7950	25. 23751
2. 23328	8. 150750	14. 165200	20. 25272	26. 119079
3. 44958	9. 221229	15. 189440	21. 66144	27. 184266
4. 105369	10. 263110	16. 10608	22. 26999	28. 378228
5. 57717	11. 128544	17. 20208	23. 226772	29. 93240
6. 33957	12. 85869	18. 13090	24. 95469	30. 19485

Exercise 5f Problems

1. 29160	4. £4081.75	7. £1124.50	10. 3000	13. 3564
2. 65280	5. 9288	8. £21.60	11. 10500	14. £52884
3. 62620	6. 7056	9. £109,200	12. 10201	15. £41.50

Exercise 5g

1. 288	5. 264	9. 492	13. 48620
2. 286	6. 1280	10. 165	14. 80601
3. 484	7. 1071	11. 640	15. 33936
4. 273	8. 961	12. 600	16. 12322

Chapter Six Subtraction by Nikhilam

Exercise 6a

1. 14	7. 334	13. 5700	19. 03	25. 2110
2. 42	8. 154	14. 4993	20. 499983	26. 35960
3. 158	9. 160	15. 0999	21. 56996	27. 019970
4. 659	10. 101	16. 29899	22. 377000	28. 56992990
5. 280	11. 6795	17. 896996	23. 3000	29. 31918999
6. 328	12. 1033	18. 564	24. 88000	30. 5999500

Exercise 6b

1. 1334	6. 779	11. 18443	16. 34889
2. 3865	7. 1899	12. 18884	17. 45712
3. 1128	8. 2889	13. 8877	18. 28788
4. 3369	9. 3835	14. 38989	19. 3889
5. 1459	10. 2667	15. 3013	20. 58999

Exercise 6c

1. 2812	**6.** 3900	**11.** 17934	**16.** 59901
2. 1691	**7.** 472	**12.** 46891	**17.** 23943
3. 1895	**8.** 7910	**13.** 18135	**18.** 14123
4. 1850	**9.** 4657	**14.** 17110	**19.** 58851
5. 5697	**10.** 3694	**15.** 33910	**20.** 48891

Exercise 6d

1. 4467	**8.** 1286	**15.** 4005	**22.** 40784	**29.** 31459
2. 1132	**9.** 339	**16.** 4214	**23.** 40086	**30.** 346
3. 5156	**10.** 119	**17.** 21022	**24.** 33875	**31.** 30078
4. 6606	**11.** 3189	**18.** 33813	**25.** 22458	**32.** 63878
5. 3168	**12.** 1849	**19.** 20185	**26.** 42889	
6. 6255	**13.** 2209	**20.** 3409	**27.** 41087	
7. 2168	**14.** 5214	**21.** 34089	**28.** 41085	

Exercise 6e

1. 41542	**6.** 419754	**11.** 117802	**16.** 186049
2. 36883	**7.** 203086	**12.** 631939	**17.** 208646
3. 61782	**8.** 34148	**13.** 350534	**18.** 270336
4. 192860	**9.** 23457	**14.** 453998	**19.** 315907
5. 488843	**10.** 757346	**15.** 136712	**20.** 528216

Exercise 6f

1. £274	**4.** £29500	**7.** 193	**10.** 2784	**13.** 2129
2. 33234	**5.** 38 cm	**8.** £1288	**11.** 379	**14.** 129
3. 5561	**6.** 244	**9.** 636	**12.** £185	**15.** £12.58

Chapter Seven Vulgar Fractions

Exercise 7a

1. $\frac{1}{5}$	**6.** $\frac{1}{6}$	**11.** $\frac{1}{10}$	**16.** $\frac{1}{20}$	**21.** $\frac{5}{7}$	**26.** $\frac{13}{20}$
2. $\frac{1}{7}$	**7.** $\frac{2}{9}$	**12.** $\frac{4}{5}$	**17.** $\frac{3}{12}$	**22.** $\frac{9}{13}$	**27.** $\frac{7}{19}$
3. $\frac{2}{3}$	**8.** $\frac{3}{7}$	**13.** $\frac{5}{6}$	**18.** $\frac{6}{11}$	**23.** $\frac{6}{11}$	**28.** $\frac{4}{15}$
4. $\frac{3}{4}$	**9.** $\frac{9}{10}$	**14.** $\frac{4}{9}$	**19.** $\frac{2}{15}$	**24.** $\frac{8}{15}$	**29.** $\frac{3}{50}$
5. $\frac{3}{5}$	**10.** $\frac{7}{12}$	**15.** $\frac{3}{8}$	**20.** $\frac{7}{8}$	**25.** $\frac{10}{17}$	**30.** $\frac{17}{100}$

Exercise 7b

1. one half
2. three quarters
3. four fifths
4. three eighths

5. two thirds
6. three fifths
7. six sevenths
8. three sixteenths

9. five eighteenths
10. one twentieth
11. two sevenths
12. one eighth

13. seven eighths
14. two ninths
15. five ninths
16. three tenths
17. nine tenths
18. four elevenths

19. eight elevenths
20. five twelfths
21. eleven twelfths
22. twelve thirteenths
23. nine fourteenths
24. thirteen fifteenths

25. eleven nineteenths
26. sixteen twenty-thirds
27. seventeen twentieths
28. twenty-one fortieths
29. twenty-seven fiftieths
30. seven hundredths

Exercise 7c

1. 2
2. 3
3. 4
4. 5
5. 6

6. 8
7. 10
8. 12
9. 15
10. 24

11. 2
12. 4
13. 9
14. 8
15. 3

16. 5
17. 7
18. 16
19. 18
20. 20

21. 25
22. 11
23. 29
24. 32
25. 36

26. 50
27. 100
28. 200
29. 250
30. 1000

Exercise 7d

1. $\frac{3}{8}$
2. $\frac{3}{4}$
3. $\frac{7}{12}$
4. $\frac{4}{9}$
5. $\frac{7}{12}$
6. $\frac{5}{6}$
7. $\frac{7}{8}$
8. $\frac{16}{36}$

Exercise 7e

1. 6
2. 8
3. 50
4. 2
5. 8

6. 4
7. 10
8. 3
9. 5
10. 7

11. 12
12. 24
13. 4
14. 20
15. 11

16. 6
17. 25
18. 1
19. 2
20. 9

21. 7 apples
22. 10 cm
23. £2.00
24. 4 pencils
25. 7 boys

26. 100 m
27. 2 cakes
28. £8.00
29. 2 plates
30. 10p

Exercise 7f

1. 15 marbles   **5.** 6 days   **9.** 60 kg   **13.** 60 runs

2. 10 marbles   **6.** $\frac{1}{3}$ **10.** 10 pearls   **14.** £6

3. 32 pages   **7.** $\frac{2}{3}$ **11.** 8 pearls

4. 9 miles   **8.** 20 kg   **12.** 2 ounces

Exercise 7g

1. $\frac{2}{4}$ **6.** $\frac{2}{5}$ **11.** $\frac{4}{7}$ **16.** $\frac{2}{9}$

2. $\frac{2}{3}$ **7.** $\frac{3}{7}$ **12.** $\frac{6}{7}$ **17.** $\frac{6}{9}$

3. $\frac{8}{9}$ **8.** $\frac{7}{12}$ **13.** $\frac{4}{10}$ **18.** $\frac{4}{5}$

4. $\frac{3}{4}$ **9.** $\frac{4}{8}$ **14.** $\frac{2}{6}$ **19.** $\frac{7}{10}$

5. $\frac{3}{5}$ **10.** $\frac{7}{9}$ **15.** $\frac{4}{5}$ **20.** $\frac{2}{8}$

Exercise 7h

1. $\frac{2}{4}$ **5.** $\frac{2}{16}$ **9.** $\frac{6}{8}$ **13.** $\frac{12}{16}$ **17.** $\frac{8}{16}$

2. $\frac{4}{4}$ **6.** $\frac{6}{8}$ **10.** $\frac{3}{8}$ **14.** $\frac{10}{16}$ **18.** $\frac{6}{8}$

3. $\frac{1}{4}$ **7.** $\frac{2}{4}$ **11.** $\frac{4}{16}$ **15.** $\frac{6}{16}$ **19.** $\frac{4}{16}$

4. $\frac{4}{8}$ **8.** $\frac{2}{8}$ **12.** $\frac{4}{8}$ **16.** $\frac{7}{8}$ **20.** $\frac{14}{16}$

Exercise 7i

1. $\frac{2}{6}$ **5.** $\frac{4}{12}$ **9.** $\frac{6}{12}$ **13.** $\frac{10}{12}$ **17.** $\frac{5}{6}$

2. $\frac{6}{6}$ **6.** $\frac{8}{12}$ **10.** $\frac{3}{6}$ **14.** $\frac{2}{6}$ **18.** $\frac{4}{12}$

3. $\frac{4}{6}$ **7.** $\frac{4}{12}$ **11.** $\frac{8}{12}$ **15.** $\frac{12}{12}$ **19.** $\frac{12}{12}$

4. $\frac{2}{12}$ **8.** $\frac{2}{6}$ **12.** $\frac{12}{12}$ **16.** $\frac{3}{3}$ **20.** $\frac{2}{3}$

Chapter Eight   Decimal Fractions

Exercise 8a

1. 2	**4.** 11	**7.** 1	**10.** 23	**13.** 25
2. 5	**5.** 16	**8.** 12	**11.** 9	**14.** 34
3. 8	**6.** 19	**9.** 7	**12.** 19	**15.** 42

16. 2	**19.** 12	**22.** 23	**25.** 231	**28.** 305
17. 5	**20.** 35	**23.** 40	**26.** 99	**29.** 219
18. 8	**21.** 1	**24.** 70	**27.** 731	**30.** 42

Exercise 8b

1. two point three	**6.** nought point two	**11.** thirty-four point five
2. four point four	**7.** three point two four	**12.** seventy-six point one
3. one point seven	**8.** five point one eight	**13.** nine point two four
4. nought point eight	**9.** nine point six three	**14.** five hundred and sixty-seven point two three
5. nought point four	**10.** two point nought five	**15.** one point four nought seven

16. 2.3	**20.** 1.05	**24.** 604.2
17. 3.7	**21.** 62.3	**25.** 0.403
18. 0.2	**22.** 50.3	
19. 5.67	**23.** 95.1	

Exercise 8c

1. 3.2	**11.** 0.7	**21.** 8.1	**31.** 5.9
2. 8.5	**12.** 3.6	**22.** 4.5	**32.** 3.4
3. 4.1	**13.** 9.3	**23.** 6.5	**33.** 5.3
4. 4.8	**14.** 9.7	**24.** 8.9	**34.** 6.6
5. 4.2	**15.** 8.9	**25.** 5.5	**35.** 9.7
6. 4.7	**16.** 3.9	**26.** 5.8	**36.** 4.9
7. 9.9	**17.** 7.3	**27.** 7.9	**37.** 5.6
8. 5.8	**18.** 1.9	**28.** 8.2	**38.** 6.6
9. 6.2	**19.** 9.9	**29.** 6.9	**39.** 7.8
10. 6.8	**20.** 6.8	**30.** 7.6	**40.** 7.9

Exercise 8d

1. 3.0	11. 4.8	21. 5.2	31. 14.0
2. 6.1	12. 9.6	22. 7.6	32. 13.2
3. 8.7	13. 8.5	23. 5.1	33. 15.5
4. 8.5	14. 8.1	24. 6.6	34. 12.0
5. 5.0	15. 7.4	25. 12.7	35. 10.0
6. 7.8	16. 7.2	26. 13.7	36. 10.0
7. 6.3	17. 6.0	27. 13.8	37. 10.0
8. 6.8	18. 9.4	28. 11.2	38. 13.4
9. 9.0	19. 9.3	29. 15.9	39. 19.6
10. 6.2	20. 5.5	30. 18.6	40. 11.2

Exercise 8e Column addition

1. 8.0	6. 9.9	11. 5.0	16. 15.12	21. 1.13	26. 1200.521
2. 7.8	7. 8.0	12. 2.3	17. 113.4	22. 1.466	27. 177.64
3. 8.1	8. 7.8	13. 6.6	18. 180.1	23. 14.593	28. 225.36
4. 8.8	9. 9.2	14. 9.9	19. 60.9	24. 9.57	29. 38.444
5. 10.0	10. 8.9	15. 22.5	20. 120.2	25. 1213.9	30. 61.167

Exercise 8f Simple subtraction

1. 7.1	11. 1.0	21. 0.2	31. 1.1
2. 2.1	12. 0.2	22. 0.2	32. 2.4
3. 1.1	13. 3.6	23. 0.5	33. 2.3
4. 1.0	14. 6.3	24. 5.2	34. 5.0
5. 0.4	15. 4.4	25. 1.5	35. 1.2
6. 2.5	16. 3.0	26. 5.0	36. 5.4
7. 1.4	17. 4.6	27. 3.4	37. 5.8
8. 1.3	18. 0.4	28. 1.0	38. 4.2
9. 2.1	19. 8.1	29. 1.5	39. 8.7
10. 1.6	20. 4.1	30. 0.0	40. 2.1

Exercise 8g

1. 10.4	4. 12.7	7. 7.2	10. 17.3
2. 5.1	5. 3.6	8. 8.2	11. 4.2
3. 7.3	6. 4.5	9. 1.1	12. 13.3

Exercise 8h Nikhilam subtraction

1. 0.8	11. 1.7	21. 1.2	31. 0.7
2. 1.9	12. 3.4	22. 0.6	32. 0.7
3. 1.5	13. 0.6	23. 2.6	33. 1.5
4. 0.4	14. 4.4	24. 4.6	34. 0.4
5. 2.3	15. 1.6	25. 1.9	35. 4.9
6. 4.8	16. 2.5	26. 2.5	36. 4.8
7. 4.9	17. 1.7	27. 2.9	37. 1.7
8. 4.5	18. 2.7	28. 2.9	38. 5.4
9. 3.5	19. 1.2	29. 1.5	39. 4.8
10. 6.7	20. 5.9	30. 6.7	40. 4.6

Exercise 8i Nikhilam subtraction

1. 12.75	7. 1.095	13. 0.168	19. 1.086	25. 7.977
2. 6.43	8. 1.679	14. 0.192	20. 0.288	26. 9.74
3. 10.84	9. 13.64	15. 2.366	21. 7.658	
4. 1.856	10. 1.566	16. 1.208	22. 11.778	
5. 0.884	11. 18.87	17. 0.118	23. 3.922	
6. 12.59	12. 1.676	18. 29.03	24. 8.808	

Exercise 8j Multiplication

1. 6.3	11. 7.2	21. 20.4	31. 18.9
2. 9.6	12. 65.1	22. 11.2	32. 32.4
3. 10.5	13. 10.5	23. 41.6	33. 15.6
4. 18.6	14. 40.8	24. 25.2	34. 15.4
5. 22.4	15. 22.4	25. 30.1	35. 69.6
6. 19.0	16. 48.6	26. 54.6	36. 60.8
7. 37.2	17. 16.0	27. 47.0	37. 15.2
8. 25.2	18. 38.5	28. 42.6	38. 65.6
9. 36.5	19. 32.8	29. 34.4	39. 50.4
10. 24.0	20. 6.0	30. 21.6	40. 22.4

Exercise 8k

1. 1.10	11. 3.69	21. 64.02	31. 3.44
2. 1.26	12. 7.70	22. 138.24	32. 14.10
3. 1.12	13. 10.08	23. 306.18	33. 392.7
4. 1.70	14. 13.02	24. 93.6	34. 219.69
5. 1.41	15. 14.72	25. 448.96	35. 25.69
6. 2.44	16. 29.76	26. 160.20	36. 3.04
7. 3.65	17. 53.20	27. 249.97	37. 5.66
8. 3.96	18. 70.74	28. 126.36	38. 66.85
9. 5.67	19. 15.36	29. 266.80	39. 127.75
10. 3.04	20. 8.90	30. 272.37	40. 5503.8

Exercise 8l

1. 20	6. 12.3	11. 7	16. 10.2
2. 340	7. 125	12. 99	17. 239
3. 2340	8. 34	13. 12.34	18. 20.05
4. 23.4	9. 45	14. 7654.5	19. 1.45
5. 74.4	10. 5	15. 457	20. 0.04

Exercise 8m

1. 200	6. 1123.4	11. 6	16. 1250
2. 3400	7. 1257.7	12. 230	17. 5630
3. 23400	8. 348.7	13. 30	18. 426.4
4. 231.4	9. 451	14. 76545	19. 14.5
5. 744.4	10. 55.4	15. 4570	20. 0.4

Exercise 8n

1. 6	6. 5.87	11. 0.05	16. 0.05
2. 34	7. 8.74	12. 2.377	17. 0.04
3. 234	8. 6.5	13. 0.126	18. 3.809
4. 40	9. 3.4	14. 48.541	19. 0.0001
5. 1.23	10. 0.3	15. 4.03	20. 0.0564

Exercise 8p

1. 3	6. 4.657	11. 0.65	16. 0.195
2. 34	7. 8.7901	12. 0.571	17. 0.053
3. 2.343	8. 2.373	13. 0.286	18. 0.008
4. 5.463	9. 0.561	14. 7.6545	19. 0.0056
5. 54.632	10. 0.7687	15. 0.045	20. 0.0009

Exercise 8q

1. 1.2	7. 1.3	13. 0.8	19. 3.171	25. 0.602
2. 2.4	8. 1.03	14. 0.5	20. 4.06	26. 0.117
3. 2.2	9. 1.07	15. 1.7	21. 0.557	27. 0.104
4. 2.3	10. 1.02	16. 1.2	22. 3.156	28. 0.286
5. 1.0	11. 3.23	17. 2.1	23. 2.13	29. 0.710
6. 4.3	12. 2.13	18. 0.5	24. 3.056	30. 75.1

Exercise 8r Writing money

1. £1.50	4. £3.12	7. £2.03	10. £2.10	13. £1.05
2. £1.40	5. £1.07	8. £5.60	11. £2.30	14. £2.07
3. £1.15	6. £1.08	9. £5.06	12. £1.01	15. £10.90

Exercise 8s Money problems

1. £12.66	4. £11.75	7. £3.25	10. £5.53
2. £3.00	5. £57.75	8. £206.00	
3. £6.15	6. £149.67	9. £2.66	

Chapter 9 The Meaning of Numbers

Exercise 9a Products

1. 6	6. 49	11. 56	16. 99	21. 32	26. 7
2. 20	7. 36	12. 12	17. 0	22. 100	27. 19
3. 24	8. 24	13. 21	18. 60	23. 800	28. 257
4. 42	9. 9	14. 48	19. 26	24. 60	29. 1
5. 0	10. 55	15. 96	20. 100	25. 12	30. 38

Exercise 9b Each number to be written as the product of two factors. Products are shown.

1. 4	**6.** 8	**11.** 36	**16.** 72	**21.** 50	**26.** 5
2. 6	**7.** 10	**12.** 30	**17.** 45	**22.** 32	**27.** 7
3. 9	**8.** 24	**13.** 25	**18.** 56	**23.** 35	**28.** 11
4. 18	**9.** 16	**14.** 40	**19.** 64	**24.** 60	**29.** 13
5. 22	**10.** 12	**15.** 55	**20.** 28	**25.** 3	**30.** 19

Exercise 9c Listing factors

1. 1×6
2×3

2. 1×8
2×4

3. 1×9
3×3

4. 1×10
2×5

5. 1×15
3×5

6. 1×14
2×7

7. 1×12
2×6
3×4

8. 1×7

9. 1×20
2×10
4×5

10. 1×18
2×9
3×6

11. 1×21
3×7

12. 1×33
3×11

13. 1×11

14. 1×5

15. 1×16
2×8
4×4

16. 1×26
2×13

17. 1×30
2×15
3×10
5×6

18. 1×35
5×7

19. 1×36
2×18
3×12
4×9
6×6

20. 1×100
2×50
4×25
5×20
10×10

Exercise 9d The Sieve of Eratosthanes

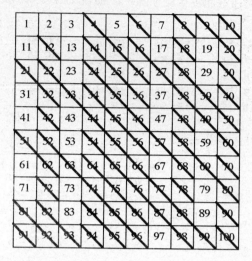

The prime numbers to 100 are:
  1, 2, 3, 5, 7, 11, 13, 17, 19, 23, 29, 31, 37, 41, 43, 47, 53, 59, 61, 67, 71, 73, 79, 83, 89, 97.

Exercise 9e Dividing by two

1. 10	**6.** 8	**11.** 21	**16.** 16
2. 25	**7.** 13	**12.** 33	**17.** 27
3. 100	**8.** 31	**13.** 42	**18.** 36
4. 12	**9.** 24	**14.** 23	**19.** 49
5. 15	**10.** 32	**15.** 44	**20.** 51

Exercise 9f Problems

1. 24	**7.** odd	**11.** 8	**16.** even
2. 2	**8.** 1 × 50	**12.** 24	**17.** odd
3. even	2 × 25		
	5 × 10	**13.** even	**18.** even
4. 3	**9.** 38	**14.** even	**19.** 46
5. 60	**10.** 29	**15.** odd	**20.** right
6. 20, 22, 24, 26, 28, 30, 32, 34			

Exercise 9g Multiples

1. 3, 6, 9, 12, 15, 18, 21, 24, 27, 30
2. 10, 20, 30, 40, 50, 60, 70, 80, 90, 100
3. 5, 10, 15, 20, 25, 30, 35, 40, 45, 50, 55, 60
4. 10, 12, 14, 16, 18, 20, 22, 24, 26, 28, 30
5. 14, 21, 28, 35, 42

6. 12, 16, 20, 24, 28, 32
7. 48, 56, 64, 72, 80, 88, 96
8. 23, 24, 25, 26, 27
9. 9, 18, 27, 36, 45
10. 48, 54, 60, 66, 72

11. 14, 16
12. 27, 30
13. 50, 55
14. 36, 42
15. 72, 81

16. 200, 250
17. 120, 140
18. 48, 54
19. 25, 20
20. 64, 80

21. 4, 8, 12, 16, 20, 24 or 28
22. 12, 24 or 36, etc
23. 30 or 60, etc
24. 15
25. 30

26. 15, 25, 35
27. 30
28. 6, 12 or 18, etc
29. 6
30. 12

Exercise 9h Multiplying by 10

1. 20
2. 50
3. 210
4. 240

5. 300
6. 160
7. 260
8. 620

9. 480
10. 640
11. 4220
12. 6600

13. 8020
14. 4060
15. 880
16. 32210

17. 54090
18. 76540
19. 12980
20. 10020

Exercise 9i Dividing by 10

1. 4
2. 6
3. 1
4. 8

5. 9
6. 34
7. 26
8. 53

9. 60
10. 79
11. 567
12. 665

13. 450
14. 400
15. 234
16. 65647

17. 53540
18. 5600
19. 76758
20. 90008

Exercise 9j Multiplying decimals by 10

1. 7.5
2. 4.6
3. 1.1
4. 4.9

5. 8.8
6. 34
7. 59
8. 51

9. 67
10. 8
11. 321
12. 416

13. 567
14. 900
15. 568
16. 213.2

17. 12.34
18. 20.67
19. 452.4
20. 760.1

Chapter Ten   Vinculums

Exercise 10a   Adding 10

1. 45	7. 253	13. 708	19. 2323	25. 10302
2. 72	8. 541	14. 802	20. 4546	26. 34528
3. 90	9. 886	15. 609	21. 7980	27. 40070
4. 31	10. 544	16. 405	22. 4010	28. 78701
5. 56	11. 688	17. 202	23. 6801	29. 13005
6. 87	12. 310	18. 1008	24. 4405	30. 100000

Exercise 10b   Subtracting 10

1. 40	7. 636	13. 496	19. 4332	25. 2995
2. 24	8. 302	14. 691	20. 9776	26. 40491
3. 66	9. 647	15. 793	21. 5420	27. 33993
4. 2	10. 866	16. 699	22. 3391	28. 49990
5. 39	11. 670	17. 194	23. 5592	29. 65694
6. 87	12. 223	18. 92	24. 4291	30. 9999

Exercise 10c   Adding 100

1. 434	7. 1087	13. 186	19. 4088	25. 87968
2. 556	8. 1772	14. 154	20. 7041	26. 55050
3. 229	9. 5974	15. 122	21. 8000	27. 12345
4. 886	10. 1100	16. 1879	22. 2021	28. 11111
5. 984	11. 2220	17. 1111	23. 6099	29. 77099
6. 1020	12. 3757	18. 1045	24. 6042	30. 100000

Exercise 10d   Subtracting 100

1. 200	7. 554	13. 5363	19. 4987	25. 19900
2. 800	8. 21	14. 3311	20. 2921	26. 68696
3. 100	9. 40	15. 6666	21. 943	27. 43151
4. 400	10. 479	16. 98665	22. 5981	28. 69900
5. 681	11. 544	17. 2922	23. 3911	29. 9999
6. 547	12. 1	18. 3910	24. 1959	30. 9900

Exercise 10e Adding 20

1. 66	7. 86	13. 933	19. 5698	25. 100
2. 92	8. 99	14. 652	20. 9125	26. 110
3. 38	9. 24	15. 136	21. 6941	27. 410
4. 56	10. 532	16. 728	22. 5555	28. 500
5. 70	11. 643	17. 982	23. 1020	29. 216
6. 43	12. 767	18. 1144	24. 5360	30. 23315

Exercise 10f Mixed practice

1. 33	11. 156	21. 600	31. 6858
2. 35	12. 785	22. 334	32. 9712
3. 255	13. 443	23. 531	33. 4000
4. 8	14. 730	24. 342	34. 6220
5. 54	15. 535	25. 645	35. 1911
6. 62	16. 159	26. 687	36. 8088
7. 87	17. 900	27. 512	37. 4966
8. 72	18. 704	28. 1012	38. 432
9. 48	19. 860	29. 87	39. 2086
10. 35	20. 804	30. 721	40. 2000

Exercise 10g Copy and complete

1. $7 = 10 - 3 = 1\overline{3}$
2. $8 = 10 - 2 = 1\overline{2}$
3. $6 = 10 - 4 = 1\overline{4}$
4. $5 = 10 - 5 = 1\overline{5}$
5. $19 = 20 - 1 = 2\overline{1}$
6. $36 = 40 - 4 = 4\overline{4}$
7. $48 = 50 - 2 = 5\overline{2}$
8. $29 = 30 - 1 = 3\overline{1}$
9. $58 = 60 - 2 = 6\overline{2}$
10. $27 = 30 - 3 = 3\overline{3}$

11. $89 = 90 - 1 = 9\overline{1}$
12. $49 = 50 - 1 = 5\overline{1}$
13. $26 = 30 - 4 = 3\overline{4}$
14. $47 = 50 - 3 = 5\overline{3}$
15. $58 = 60 - 2 = 6\overline{2}$
16. $28 = 30 - 2 = 3\overline{2}$
17. $39 = 40 - 1 = 4\overline{1}$
18. $77 = 80 - 3 = 8\overline{3}$
19. $37 = 40 - 3 = 4\overline{3}$
20. $68 = 70 - 2 = 7\overline{2}$

Exercise 10h Copy and complete

1. $1\bar{3} = 10 - 3 = 7$
2. $2\bar{7} = 20 - 7 = 13$
3. $3\bar{8} = 30 - 8 = 22$
4. $4\bar{9} = 40 - 9 = 41$
5. $5\bar{6} = 50 - 6 = 44$
6. $7\bar{8} = 70 - 8 = 62$
7. $9\bar{3} = 90 - 3 = 87$
8. $8\bar{1} = 80 - 1 = 79$
9. $9\bar{7} = 90 - 7 = 83$
10. $8\bar{4} = 80 - 4 = 76$

11. $2\bar{1} = 20 - 1 = 19$
12. $9\bar{1} = 90 - 1 = 89$
13. $6\bar{4} = 60 - 4 = 56$
14. $2\bar{3} = 20 - 3 = 17$
15. $5\bar{8} = 50 - 8 = 42$
16. $6\bar{8} = 60 - 8 = 52$
17. $7\bar{3} = 70 - 3 = 67$
18. $8\bar{3} = 80 - 3 = 77$
19. $7\bar{1} = 70 - 1 = 69$
20. $6\bar{3} = 60 - 3 = 57$

Exercise 10i Changing units digits into vinculums

1. $3\bar{3}$
2. $4\bar{1}$
3. $3\bar{2}$
4. $2\bar{3}$
5. $8\bar{1}$
6. $2\bar{2}$
7. $2\bar{4}$
8. $3\bar{4}$
9. $8\bar{3}$
10. $9\bar{2}$
11. $5\bar{1}$
12. $9\bar{1}$
13. $3\bar{4}$
14. $5\bar{2}$
15. $6\bar{4}$
16. $3\bar{5}$
17. $5\bar{3}$
18. $4\bar{3}$
19. $5\bar{4}$
20. $9\bar{3}$
21. $6\bar{1}$
22. $2\bar{1}$
23. $7\bar{1}$
24. $7\bar{4}$
25. $6\bar{5}$
26. $4\bar{1}$
27. $6\bar{3}$
28. $3\bar{1}$
29. $4\bar{2}$
30. $1\bar{1}$

Exercise 10j Changing numbers back to their ordinary form.

1. 32
2. 18
3. 2
4. 47
5. 88
6. 35
7. 45
8. 48
9. 36
10. 49
11. 28
12. 46
13. 65
14. 29
15. 38
16. 58
17. 78
18. 66
19. 75
20. 89
21. 55
22. 69
23. 25
24. 67
25. 37
26. 26
27. 57
28. 76
29. 42
30. 59
31. 68
32. 77
33. 287
34. 765
35. 479
36. 156
37. 448
38. 638
39. 386
40. 228

Exercise 10k Changing the tens digit into a vinculum number.

1. 4$\bar{2}$1	7. 6$\bar{4}$2	13. 54$\bar{1}$3	19. 2$\bar{2}$4	25. 1$\bar{1}$3
2. 3$\bar{3}$8	8. 4$\bar{3}$1	14. 13$\bar{2}$0	20. 21$\bar{3}$3	26. 1$\bar{2}$4
3. 7$\bar{1}$0	9. 24$\bar{1}$1	15. 44$\bar{4}$1	21. 33$\bar{4}$4	27. 1$\bar{3}$4
4. 3$\bar{4}$1	10. 12$\bar{3}$0	16. 45$\bar{4}$2	22. 25$\bar{1}$5	28. 1$\bar{1}$1
5. 6$\bar{2}$2	11. 34$\bar{4}$1	17. 11$\bar{2}$2	23. 3$\bar{2}$2	29. 1$\bar{2}$0
6. 5$\bar{1}$3	12. 44$\bar{2}$2	18. 21$\bar{3}$3	24. 5$\bar{4}$1	30. 1$\bar{1}$0

Exercise 10l Change each tens vinculum digit back into an ordinary number.

1. 373	7. 898	13. 1195	19. 12081	25. 193
2. 481	8. 786	14. 4291	20. 5465	26. 65
3. 692	9. 284	15. 8663	21. 6666	27. 56
4. 457	10. 372	16. 7589	22. 65392	28. 7083
5. 272	11. 683	17. 5390	23. 70684	29. 6688
6. 676	12. 771	18. 3272	24. 54396	30. 1091

Exercise 10m Change each vinculum digit back into an ordinary number.

1. 3929	7. 1929	13. 8392	19. 36327	25. 181822
2. 4837	8. 3718	14. 23716	20. 49229	26. 392931
3. 916	9. 4949	15. 20809	21. 41718	27. 300809
4. 3607	10. 3636	16. 30647	22. 504937	28. 160910
5. 4938	11. 2727	17. 55281	23. 37092	29. 574555
6. 5746	12. 6949	18. 46282	24. 290911	30. 8217

Exercise 10n Changing digits which are more than five into vinculums

1. 4$\overline{2}$2	7. 4$\overline{3}$3$\overline{2}$	13. 4$\overline{1}$22$\overline{2}$	19. 11$\overline{2}$2$\overline{4}$	25. 2$\overline{3}$3$\overline{4}$
2. 2$\overline{1}$3	8. 2$\overline{3}$3$\overline{3}$	14. 5$\overline{2}$11$\overline{1}$	20. 33$\overline{4}$2$\overline{2}$	26. 35$\overline{2}$
3. 4$\overline{3}$3	9. 3$\overline{2}$1$\overline{1}$	15. 4$\overline{3}$2$\overline{1}$0	21. 3$\overline{2}$12$\overline{1}$	27. 3$\overline{1}$2$\overline{2}$1
4. 23$\overline{1}$	10. 5$\overline{4}$45	16. 3$\overline{2}$11$\overline{4}$	22. 33$\overline{4}\overline{4}$1	28. 33$\overline{4}$2$\overline{4}$
5. 33$\overline{3}$	11. 4$\overline{2}$21	17. 3$\overline{3}$32$\overline{4}$	23. 5$\overline{1}$2$\overline{3}$2	29. 22$\overline{5}$2$\overline{2}$
6. 41$\overline{4}$	12. 352$\overline{2}$	18. 2$\overline{1}$4$\overline{2}$2	24. 34$\overline{2}$3$\overline{1}$	30. 45$\overline{4}$1$\overline{1}$

Exercise 10p Adding and subtracting vinculum numbers

1. $\overline{5}$	11. $\overline{2}$	21. $\overline{9}$	31. 5
2. $\overline{2}$	12. $\overline{3}$	22. $\overline{4}$	32. 6
3. $\overline{4}$	13. $\overline{5}$	23. $\overline{6}$	33. 5
4. $\overline{7}$	14. $\overline{1}$	24. $\overline{3}$	34. 2
5. $\overline{3}$	15. $\overline{2}$	25. $\overline{8}$	35. 4
6. $\overline{6}$	16. $\overline{3}$	26. $\overline{4}$	36. 5
7. $\overline{6}$	17. $\overline{3}$	27. $\overline{7}$	37. 1
8. $\overline{6}$	18. $\overline{4}$	28. $\overline{9}$	38. 0
9. $\overline{6}$	19. 0	29. 0	39. 8
10. $\overline{8}$	20. $\overline{2}$	30. $\overline{1}$	40. 13

Chapter 11 Algebra

1. 25	11. 235	21. 5319034534
2. 95	12. 2230	22. 125
3. 18	13. 5553	23. 1445193
4. 933	14. 999	24. 323540013
5. 74	15. 20153	25. 5000500
6. 75	16. 4135	26. 9999
7. 505	17. 850	27. 12358
8. 408	18. 053	28. 987654321
9. 9030	19. 412499	29. 200000000002
10. 232	20. 39432	30. 435435435435

Exercise 11c

1. 7	11. 4	21. 6	31. 4
2. 10	12. 19	22. 1	32. 3
3. 15	13. 315	23. 6	33. 6
4. 24	14. 0	24. 4	34. 0
5. 100	15. 8	25. 1	35. 8
6. 4	16. 5	26. 4	36. 9
7. 1	17. 12	27. 14	37. 18
8. 0	18. 14	28. 5	38. 4
9. 5	19. 5	29. 16	39. 100
10. 4	20. 0	30. 4	40. 25

Exercise 11d

1. 6	11. 300	21. 8	31. 22
2. 12	12. 18	22. 14	32. 0
3. 24	13. 33	23. 18	33. 50
4. 21	14. 60	24. 4	34. 24
5. 3	15. 36	25. 10	35. 60
6. 0	16. 27	26. 12	36. 18
7. 15	17. 18	27. 6	37. 26
8. 9	18. 24	28. 20	38. 16
9. 27	19. 42	29. 2	39. 28
10. 30	20. 12	30. 16	40. 28

Exercise 11e

1. 8	11. 600	21. 9	31. 17
2. 8	12. 17	22. 1	32. 12
3. 30	13. 64	23. 5	33. 28
4. 42	14. 30	24. 5	34. 4
5. 8	15. 54	25. 5	35. 19
6. 16	16. 5	26. 15	
7. 20	17. 7	27. 7	
8. 99	18. 6	28. 13	
9. 18	19. 2	29. 8	
10. 72	20. 1	30. 19	

Exercise 11f

1. 3	5. 1	9. 5	13. 8
2. 2	6. 20	10. 35	14. 27
3. 6	7. 8	11. 9	15. 8
4. 4	8. 7	12. 2	16. x

Exercise 11g

1. 18	11. 30	21. 7	31. 13
2. 17	12. 17	22. 0	32. 27
3. 50	13. 6	23. 9	33. 30
4. 52	14. 5	24. 9	34. 6
5. 75	15. 125	25. 1	35. 6
6. 201	16. 3	26. 2	36. 21
7. 4	17. 5	27. 35	
8. 100	18. 2	28. 11	
9. 32	19. 6	29. 30	
10. 1	20. 17	30. 27	

Exercise 11h

1. 3	7. 13	13. 100	19. 0	25. 30
2. 3	8. 12	14. 1	20. 7	26. 9
3. 7	9. 25	15. 350	21. 12	27. 12
4. 12	10. 95	16. 3	22. 9	28. 8
5. 0	11. 0	17. 2	23. 4	29. 31
6. 2	12. 34	18. 1	24. 10	30. 201

Exercise 11i

1. 0	7. 12	13. 15	19. 55	25. 1000
2. 5	8. 13	14. 13	20. 86	26. 51
3. 5	9. 19	15. 6	21. 33	27. 30
4. 18	10. 45	16. 6	22. 70	28. 120
5. 11	11. 64	17. 8	23. 29	29. 1
6. 5	12. 7	18. 53	24. 60	30. 339

Exercise 11j

1. 8	4. 5	7. 10	10. 15	13. 14
2. 39	5. 0	8. 2	11. 22	14. 622
3. 5	6. 6	9. 22	12. 24	15. 801

Exercise 11k

1. 3	8. 5	15. 9	22. 8	29. 8
2. 4	9. 0	16. 11	23. 3	30. 12
3. 1	10. 4	17. 10	24. 3	31. 9
4. 2	11. 2	18. 7	25. 2	32. 1
5. 3	12. 4	19. 2	26. 3	
6. 2	13. 12	20. 6	27. 4	
7. 7	14. 8	21. 8	28. 8	

Exercise 11l

1. $4a$	11. $8a$	21. $9x$	31. $6a$	41. $14d$
2. $5b$	12. $5p$	22. $6h$	32. $8x$	42. 0
3. $6c$	13. $7g$	23. $10a$	33. $17h$	43. $4s$
4. $7h$	14. $10y$	24. $5m$	34. 0	44. f
5. $12s$	15. $9b$	25. $11p$	35. $6d$	45. $3k$
6. $13p$	16. $4n$	26. $14z$	36. $10b$	46. $6n$
7. $45t$	17. $9x$	27. $10b$	37. $28m$	47. $2x$
8. $12q$	18. $12d$	28. $12y$	38. $3x$	48. v
9. $34f$	19. $11e$	29. $16c$	39. $5y$	49. p
10. $37m$	20. $10k$	30. $100x$	40. $5w$	50. $9t$
				51. $36z$